Hinduism and Its Sense of History

Hinduism and Its Sense of History

ARVIND SHARMA

OXFORD
UNIVERSITY PRESS

OXFORD
UNIVERSITY PRESS

YMCA Library Building, Jai Singh Road, New Delhi 110 001

Oxford University Press is a department of the University of Oxford. It furthers the University's objective of excellence in research, scholarship, and education by publishing worldwide in

Oxford New York

Auckland Bangkok Buenos Aires Cape Town Chennai
Dar es Salaam Delhi Hong Kong Istanbul Karachi Kolkata
Kuala Lumpur Madrid Melbourne Mexico City Mumbai Nairobi
São Paulo Shanghai Taipei Tokyo Toronto

Oxford is a registered trade mark of Oxford University Press in the UK and in certain other countries

Published in India
By Oxford University Press, New Delhi

First published 2003

ISBN 0 19 566531 7

Printed by Rashtriya Printers, Delhi 110 032
Published by Manzar Khan, Oxford University Press
YMCA Library Building, Jai Singh Road, New Delhi 110 001

For

Dr Vidya Niwas Misra

Contents

Acknowledgement

Research leading to this book was undertaken while the author was the Infinity Foundation Visiting Professor of Indic Studies at Harvard University in the Spring of 2001.

History of the Notion that Hinduism Has No Sense of History

I

The view that Hinduism as a religion, or the Hindus as a people, lack a sense of history has been expressed so often as to have become a cliché.[1] Even when scholars have tried to take a more sophisticated as opposed to a clichéd view, the effect has often been to reinforce it. Professor A. L. Basham, for instance, would concede to the Hindus a sense of the past, but still not of history.[2] Elsewhere he allows for a sense of antiquity as well, if only to suggest that Hinduism possessed an exaggerated sense of it,[3] while some have argued that Hinduism possessed a sense of historical pessimism[4] but, again, not of history.

Even when scholars take a more nuanced view and distinguish between: (1) lack of chronology,[5] (2) lack of history,[6] (3) a lack of a sense of history,[7] (4) a lack of historiography,[8] and (5) the lack of a theory of history,[9] the net effect is the same. The alleged lack of historiography and a theory of history in India only buttresses the previous claim of a lack of a sense of history, while its abundant history makes the lack of a sense of it only stand out more starkly.

Similarly, when Hinduism is compared to other religions of Indian origin, such as Buddhism, Jainism or Sikhism, it suffers by this comparison, in the sense that these latter religions are usually represented as being endowed, at least relatively to Hinduism, with a greater or better sense of history. It is then noted that the Mahāvaṁśa and the Dīpavaṁśa record the history of Buddhism in Śrī Laṅkā,[10] the death of Lord Mahāvīra initiates a historical era in Jainism,[11] and not only is Sikhism's history relatively recent and well documented,[12] a sense of history within it is also more manifest.[13]

Although the claim that Hindus lack a sense of history has gained the virtual status of an Indological axiom in modern times, the view can also be traced back to medieval times, and to a certain extent even to ancient times.

The explicit or tacit assessment that Hindus lack a sense of history is likely to come from a people who, by comparison, possess it. One therefore thinks naturally of the encounter of the Greeks with India, for 'what is remarkable about the Greeks is not the fact that their historical thought combined a residue of elements which we would call non-historical but the fact that side by side with these it contained elements of what we call history'.[14] Thus the invasion of India by Alexander in 326 BC, a decisive moment in this encounter, takes on not merely a historical but historiographic significance as well, not the least because of the numerous hands which chronicled it and because of the Graeco-Roman tradition of recounting it in Late Antiquity.[15]

These accounts, in so far as they are concerned not with the description of the details of Alexander's expedition but with the description of Indic civilization as such, draw on the *Indica* of Megasthenes. Megasthenes is said to have served as the Seleucid ambassador at the court of Candragupta Maurya in the fourth century BC and left a detailed account based on his sojourn called *Indica*. The *Indica* as such is not extant, but has been partially reconstructed by collecting and collating the passages cited from it, directly or indirectly, by later writers.[16]

Its testimony seems to display two strands on the sense of history as found in ancient India. In one context it speaks, not of a lack of a sense of history, but of history as such, in India. Fragment 46 reads:

> But what just reliance can we place on the accounts of India from such expeditions as those of Kyros and Semiramis? Megasthenes concurs in this view, and recommends his readers to *put no faith in the history of India*. Its people, he says, never sent an expedition abroad, nor was their country ever invaded and conquered except by Herakles and Dionysos in old times, and by the Makedonians in our own.[17]

One can see here the germ of the idea that the ancient Indians lacked a sense of history, an idea destined to achieve remarkable extensions in the future. Thus H. G. Rawlinson is led into remarking that 'of the ancient history of India, Megasthenes apparently learnt nothing worth recording, save legends of a monarch whom he identified with Bacchus or Herakles.

This is not surprising, as the science of history was always entirely neglected by the Hindus.'[18] We shall discover later that this is not quite so. In this present context, however, Megasthenes connects it with India's dealings with the countries beyond India. The view held here—that Indians never militarily crossed the borders of their country and conquered another country—contributed to another standard view of Indian history—that Indian history is a history of invasions of India, but never by India. Megasthenes seems to be promoting such a perspective and seems to be saying that as Indians did not mount any such invasions, there could possibly be no historical account of such invasions. This point should be distinguished from whether one possessed a historical record of the history of India *as such*. Indeed, in the context of dealing with Indians in India, Megasthenes takes a different tack; and speaks of the ancient history of the Indians. What is striking in this respect is the fact that the account of the political history supplied by these Indians (Hindus?) to Megasthenes is restrained rather than fabulous in terms of the time periods involved. The following surviving fragments from the *Indica* of Megasthenes form the basis of this judgment:

Of the Ancient History of the Indians

For the Indians stand almost alone among the nations in never having migrated from their own country. From the days of Father Bacchus to Alexander the Great their kings are reckoned at 154, whose reigns extend over 6451 years and 3 months.

Solin. 52.5

Father Bacchus was the first who invaded India, and was the first of all who triumphed over the vanquished Indians. From him to Alexander the Great 6451 years are reckoned with 3 months additional, the calculation being made by counting the kings who reigned in the intermediate period, to the number of 153.[19]

Arrian (second century) supplies more details.

From the time of Dionysus to Sandracottus the Indians counted 153 kings and a period of 6402 years, but among these a republic was thrice established ... and another to 300 years, and another to 120 years. The Indians also tell us that Dionysus was earlier than Heracles by fifteen generations, and that except him no one made a hostile invasion of India—not even Cyrus the son of Cambyses, although he undertook an expedition against the Scythians, and otherwise showed himself the most enterprising monarch in all Asia; but that Alexander indeed came and overthrew in war all whom he attacked, and would even have conquered the whole world had his army been willing to follow him. On the other hand, a sense of justice, they say, prevented any Indian king from attempting conquest beyond the limits of India.[20]

It is noteworthy that the European translators like J. W. McCrindle were themselves struck by the moderation of the numbers involved, when viewed in the background of the cosmological durations associated with the doctrines of the Yugas.[21] As P. V. Kane points out, these passages are:

> of very great importance for one reason, viz. that it proves that in the 4th century BC there was a persistent Indian tradition which carried back Indian civilization and ordered government to 6000 years before the 4th century BC.[22]

The invasion of Alexander was followed by the invasions of the Bactrian Greeks, the Śakas, the Parthians and the Kuṣāṇas. This is the so-called age of invasions, which intervenes between the periods of the Maurya and the Gupta dynasty in the history of ancient India. These invasions, as A. L. Basham puts it, are 'all inadequately documented',[23] and offer little cultural comment except by way of emphasizing the prevailing political disunity in India. However, this period is an outstanding one in terms of chronology. A. L. Basham notes:

> Until the 1st century BC there is no good evidence that India had any regular system of recording the year of an event by dating in a definite era like the A.U.C. of Rome or the Christian era of medieval and modern Europe. Early inscriptions are dated if at all in the regnal year of the ruling king. The idea of dating over a long period of time from a fixed year was almost certainly introduced into India by the invaders of North-West, who have left the earliest inscriptions thus dated in India. Unfortunately, the Indians did not adopt a uniform era, and a number of systems of dating were in use from that time onwards.[24]

The two such continuous eras—the Vikrama Era (58 BC) and the Śaka Era (78 BC), which are still current in India,[25] date from this period. This phenomenon may contain a historical comment by implication—that India had not until this period evolved a system of reckoning events from a fixed point. A lack of a sense of chronology in this sense went hand in hand with a lack of sense of history.[26]

II

One may turn next to the evidence left by the Chinese travellers to India on the presence or absence of a historical sense among the Hindus. Not enough critical attention has been paid to their accounts from this point of view, despite the high standing enjoyed by historiography in Chinese culture.[27]

One consequence of the spread of Buddhism in China from the beginning of the Christian era onwards was the increased movements of Buddhist scholars and pilgrims between India and China. For instance, 'in 972 AD, 43 Buddhist monks from Western India reached Ch'ang-An.'[28]

Similarly, according to accounts preserved in Chinese texts, '60 Chinese monks (including some of Korean and Central Asian origin) visited India during the latter half of the seventh century AD.'[29] The best known among these Chinese travelers who had begun visiting India even earlier are Faxian, Xuanzang, and Yijing, whose accounts of their visits to India are an important source of ancient India's history. We turn now to an examination of these accounts.

Faxian travelled through India and Śrī Laṅkā in search of a copy of the Vinaya text from AD 399–414, that is, during the Gupta period of Indian history. The main focus of his interest was Buddhism. It is striking in this context that he is said to place the date of Buddha's Parinirvāṇa in 1050 BC.[30] The Sect of the Three Stages in China places Buddha's Parinirvana in 949 BC, for perhaps sectarian reasons.[31] It is nevertheless a curious fact that these dates are neglected in favour of the Canton record, which confirms the tendency to place the date around 486 BC.[32] Faxian himself does not even mention the name of the king during whose reign he travelled through the Middle Kingdom, perhaps because his interests were pious rather than political but he mentions two facts, which have a bearing on our topic. At one point, while describing the Middle Kingdom, he writes:

> After Buddha attained to pari-nirvāṇa the kings of the various countries and the heads of the Vaiśyas built vihāras for the priests, and endowed them with fields, houses, gardens, and orchards, along with the resident populations and their cattle, the grants being engraved on the plates of metal, so that afterwards they were handed down from king to king, without any one daring to annul them, and they remain even to the present time.[33]

The records of grants on durable material is specially worth noting, because it contrasts sharply with the absence of the use of such material to preserve the Vinaya texts Faxian (=Fa-hien) was scouting around India for. His luck, however, changed in Patna.

> From Vārāṇasī (the travellers) went back east to Pāṭaliputra. Fā-hien's original object had been to search for (copies of) the Vinaya. In the various kingdoms of North India, however, he had found one master transmitting orally (the rules) to another, but no written copies, which he could transcribe. He had therefore travelled far and come on to Central India. Here, in the mahāyāna monastery, he found a copy of the Vinaya, containing the Mahāsaṅghika rules,—those which were observed in the first Great Council, while Buddha was still in the world. The original copy was

handed down in the Jetavana vihāra. As to the other eighteen schools, each one has the views and decisions of its own masters. Those agree (with this) in the general meaning, but they have small and trivial differences, as when one opens and another shuts. This copy (of the rules), however, is the most complete, with the fullest explanations.[34]

This second piece of evidence confirms the preponderance of oral transmission among the religieux, so much so that many Jaina texts were lost because those who knew them perished in a famine.[35] The first piece of evidence however indicates the careful preservation of grants in writing in a secular context.

Xuanzang is the more famous visitor from China, who stayed in India during the time of King Harṣa (r. 606–47).[36] He testifies to the fact that there was a tradition of maintaining detailed records in the provinces. He writes:

With respect to the records of events, each province has its own official for preserving them in writing. The record of these events in their full character is called *Ni-lo-pi-ch'a* (Nīlapiṭa, *blue deposit)*. In these records are mentioned good and evil events, with calamities and fortunate occurrences.[37]

But even more remarkable, from the point of view of assessing the historical sense of the Hindus, is the record of his first conversation with King Harṣa, which contains a reference to King Harṣa (under the title Śīlāditya) and to King Kumārarāja of Kāmarūpa (modern Assam).

At this time Śīlāditya-rāja was visiting different parts of his empire, and found himself at Kie-mi-ou-ki-lo, when he gave the following order to Kumāra-rāja: 'I desire you to come at once to the assembly with the strange Śramaṇa you are entertaining at the Nālanda convent.' On this, coming with Kumāra-rāja, we attended the assembly. The king, Śīlāditya, after the fatigue of the journey was over, said, 'From what country do you come, and what do you seek in your travels?'

He said in reply, 'I come from the great Tang country, and I ask permission to seek for the law (*religious books*) of Buddha.'

The king said, 'Whereabouts is the great Tang country? by what road do you travel? and is it far from this, or near?'

In reply he said, 'My country lies to the northeast from this several myriads of li; it is the kingdom which in India is called Mahāchina.'

The king answered, 'I have heard that the country of Mahāchina has a king called Ts'in, the son of heaven, when young distinguished for his spiritual abilities, when old then (called) "divine warrior." The empire in former generations was in disorder and confusion, everywhere divided and in disunion; soldiers were in conflict, and all the people were afflicted with calamity. Then the king of Ts'in, son of heaven, who had conceived from the first vast purposes, brought into exercise all his pity and love;

he brought about a right understanding, and pacified and settled all within the seas. His laws and instruction spread on every side. People from other countries brought under his influence declared themselves ready to submit to his rule. The multitude whom he nourished generously sang in their songs of the prowess of the king of Ts'in. I have learned long since his praises and sung thus in verse. Are the records (*laudatory hymns*) of his great (*complete*) qualities well founded? Is this the king of the great Tang, of which you speak?'

Replying, he said, 'China is the country of our former kings, but the "great Tang" is the country of our present ruler. Our king in former times, before he became hereditary heir to the throne (*before the empire was established*), was called the sovereign of Ts'in, but now he is called the "king of heaven" (*emperor*). At the end of the former dynasty the people had no ruler, civil war raged on every hand and caused confusion, the people were destroyed, when the king of Ts'in, by his supernatural gifts, exercised his love and compassion on every hand; by his power the wicked were destroyed on every side, the eight regions found rest, and the ten thousand kingdoms brought tribute. He cherished creatures of every kind, submitted with respect to the three precious ones. He lightened the burdens of the people and mitigated punishment, so that the country abounded in resources and the people enjoyed complete rest. It would be difficult to recount all the great changes he accomplished.'

Śīlāditya-rāja replied, 'Very excellent indeed! the people are happy in the hands of such a holy king.'[38]

The third famous Chinese pilgrim who visited India was Yijing, his trip inspired in part by the example of Xuanzang. Yijing also basically deals with matters of Buddhist interest but at two points his remarks and observations become significant for our study. One of them describes the fate of the students after they have successfully obtained their degree.

Thus instructed by their teachers and instructing others they pass two or three years, generally in the Nālanda monastery in Central India, or in the country of Valabhī (Walā) in Western India. These two places are like Chin-ma, Shih-ch'ü, Lung-mên, and Ch'ue-li in China, and there eminent and accomplished men assemble in crowds, discuss possible and impossible doctrines, and after having been assured of the excellence of their opinions by wise men, become far famed for their wisdom. To try the sharpness of their wit (lit. 'sharp point of the sword'), they proceed to the king's court to lay down before it the sharp weapon (of their abilities); there they present their schemes and show their (political) talent, seeking to be appointed in the practical government. When they are present in the House of Debate, they raise their seat and seek to prove their wonderful cleverness.

When they are refuting heretic doctrines all their opponents become tongue-tied and acknowledge themselves undone. Then the sound of their fame makes the five mountains (of India) vibrate, and their renown flows, as it were, over the four borders. They receive grants of land, and are advanced to a high rank; *their famous names are*, as a reward, *written* in white on their lofty gates. After this they can follow whatever occupation they like.[39]

Two points are of special interest here. First of all, Yijing seems to be referring here to bureaucrat-scholars, not quite the *mandarins* of his own land, but not recluses either. Moreover, this active engagement of scholars in political life presumably involved the presence of a historical sense. At the same time the passage seems to provide a clue to the absence of written accounts, by pointing to the highly oral nature of the intellectual engagement. Elsewhere he testifies to this in even stronger terms when he writes:

... In India there are two traditional ways in which one can attain to great intellectual power. Firstly, by repeatedly committing to memory the intellect is developed; secondly, the alphabet fixes one's ideas. By this way, after the practice of ten days or a month, a student feels his thoughts rise like a fountain, and can commit to memory whatever he has once heard [not requiring to be told twice], this is far from being a myth, for I myself have met such men.[40]

It is significant that although the Chinese pilgrims do indicate a reliance on the spoken rather than the written word, they do not criticize the Hindus for lacking a sense of history.

One wonders to what extent the charge of a lack of historical sense is implicated in the political relationships between the parties involved. The charge was levelled in its full-blown form by Al-Bīrūnī, and was then given an extra bounce by European scholarship, in both cases at a time when India and the Hindus were entering into a ruler-ruled relationship of subordination and even of inferiority. From the perspective of Islamic civilization the Hindus were idolaters, and that of Christian-European civilization, pagans or uncivilized. The extent to which the specific charge of a lack of historical sense is a reflection of a more generally negative attitude towards Hindu civilization is difficult to pin down but should not, on that account, be completely overlooked. From this point of view, it might not be an accident that the history-conscious Chinese, who do not accuse the Hindus of lacking a sense of history, were also people who, at that point in history, tended to think highly of India (some reservations notwithstanding). The following passage conveys some of the feelings involved on both sides, which seem essentially positive.

When Fa-sien [=Faxian] and Tao-ching first arrived at the Jetavana monastery, and thought how the World-honoured one had formerly resided there for twenty-five years, painful reflections arose in their minds. Born in a border-land, along with their like-minded friends, they had travelled through so many kingdoms; some of those friends had returned (to their own land), and some had (died), proving the impermanence and uncertainty of life; and to-day they saw the place where Buddha had lived now unoccupied by him. They were melancholy through their pain of heart, and the crowd of monks came out, and asked them from what kingdom they were come. 'We are come,' they replied, 'from the land of Han.' 'Strange,' said the monks with a sigh, 'that men of a border country should be able to come here in search of our Law!' Then they said to one another, 'During all the time that we, preceptors and monks, have succeeded to one another, we have never seen men of Han, followers of our system, arrive here.'[41]

The case of Xuanzang hardly requires further documentation, while the following passage from Yijing speaks for itself:

(Note by I-tsing [=Yijing]): Even in the island of Pulo Condore (in the south) and in the country of Sūli (in the north), people praise the Sanskrit Sutras, how much more then should people of the Divine Land (China), as well as the Celestial Store House (India), teach the real rules of the language! Thus the people of India said in praise (*of China*): 'The wise Mañjuśrī is at present in Ping Chou, where the people are greatly blessed by his presence. We ought therefore to respect and admire that country, &c.'

The whole of their account is too long to be produced.[42]

The cordial relations are further confirmed by the statement of Yijing that a King Mahārāja Śrī Gupta built a temple near Mṛgaśikhāvana 'which was about forty yojanas east of Nālandā, following the course of the Ganges',[43] for the comfort of Chinese pilgrims. This king is sometimes identified with the founder of the Gupta Dynasty. 'It was handsomely endowed and at the time of I-tsing's itinerary (673–95 AD) its dilapidated remnants were known as the 'Temple of China'.[44]

III

It is with the arrival of the Muslims on the Indian scene that the Hindus are charged with lacking a sense of both chronology and history for the first time in full measure. It is found in Al-Bīrūnī's famous work, often abbreviated as *Tahkīk-i-Hind*,[45] and known in short as 'Alberuni's India' after the title of its English translation by Edward C. Sachau. He writes:

Unfortunately the Indians do not pay much attention to the historical order of things, they are very careless in relating the chronological succession of their kings, and when they are pressed for information and are at a loss, not knowing what to say, they invariably take to tale-telling. But for this, we should communicate to the reader the traditions, which we have received from some people among them.[46]

Incidents that occurred during the period of Islamic rule sometimes confirm this picture. For instance, 'when the records of Aśoka first came to notice towards the close of the eighteenth century AD, their script was as much an enigma to all as it was in the fourteenth century AD when the emperor Firuz Tughlak brought a pillar with Aśoka's inscription to Delhi, and made a vain attempt to have it read by the Indian Pundits.'[47] The incident is worth recording, because it seems that the knowledge of the script was already lost in a period far anterior to the fourteenth century, even as early as the fourth century.

The Chinese travellers, Fa-hsien [=Faxian] and Yuan Chwang [=Xuanzang] for instance, who visited India in the fourth and the seventh century AD respectively, could not find local experts to help them to a right reading of the Aśokan edicts they came across. They have recorded wrong readings of the inscriptions they saw, the results of mere guesswork or hearsay information from local people not confessing to their own ignorance of the script. Indeed, the decipherment of Aśokan script is a romance of modern scholarship.[48]

Given the importance of Aśoka in the reconstruction of ancient Indian history, and the Aśokan edicts in reconstructing the reign of Aśoka, it might be of interest to consider John Strong's observation that 'it has been customary in scholarly circles, to read and interpret the legends of Aśoka in the light of the edicts. In the history of Buddhism, however, just the opposite happened; the pillars and inscriptions were explained in view of the legends.'[49] Xuanzang provides an interesting example here:

Another instance of the way the legends of Aśoka have affected the interpretation of the edicts may be found in the pilgrim's account of a pillar edict at a site near Pāṭaliputra. Not too far from the city, Yuan Chwang declares, 'there was a stone pillar about thirty feet high, with an inscription much injured. The sum of the contents of the inscription was that Aśoka, strong in faith, had thrice given Jambudvīpa as a religious offering to the Buddhist order, and thrice redeemed it.' Yuan Chwang's misreading of the inscription makes perfect sense to one familiar with the legends of Aśoka. For, in the legends Aśoka is indeed portrayed, several times, as offering the whole world and his own sovereignty to the Buddhist Saṅgha, and on one of these occasions, at the end of his life, he is even said to have made a written inscription recording his gift and testifying to his generosity and devotion. Thus, the Chinese pilgrims may well have been misinterpreting the Aśokan edicts, but they were misrepresenting them in the light of what they knew about Aśoka from the legends. It is understandable, then, that when James Prinsep deciphered the Brāhmī script in

1837 and correctly read the edicts, he did not know whose they were. Misled by Aśoka's use in his inscriptions of the name. 'Beloved of the Gods' (Devānāmpriya) he claimed the pillars had been erected by King Devānāmpriya Tissa of Śrī Laṅkā. Shortly thereafter, George Turnour corrected him and rightly attributed the edicts to Aśoka. Interestingly enough, he did this on the basis of his knowledge of the Pali legends that also call Aśoka 'Devānāmpiya'. Once again, the legends were influencing the reading of the edicts.[50]

IV

The establishment of British rule in India, after the British success at the battle of Plassey in 1757, provides the context for a shift of perspective from the Islamic to the European—and shifting perspectives within the European perspectives as well. The Hindus' sense of history came up for consideration towards the end of the eighteenth century. The Asiatic Society of Bengal had already been founded on the 'first day of 1784' and the results of its investigation into the history of India began the process of what has been called the discovery of ancient India. William Jones (1746–94), a pioneer in the field, made history by proposing the identification of Sandrocottus of the Greek accounts with Candragupta Maurya of the Mauryan dynasty. The basis of making this connection in retrospect appears rather rude. He identified Candragupta Maurya on the basis of a Sanskrit drama in which he is a prime character, namely, the *Mudrārakṣasa* of Viśākhadatta, with which he had now become familiar. Nevertheless the identification has stood the test of time, and enabled the setting up of the chronological scaffolding of ancient Indian history.

At the same time it must be added that India's claim to antiquity caused some problems in Christian circles, in which the date of creation as determined by Bishop Usher, as having occurred in 4004 BC was still considered authoritative. As P. J. Marshall observes, 'British public opinion was not prepared to accept a chronology which would be damaging to orthodox Christian belief.'[51] European imagination in this respect was destined to become liberated only in the next century. Even in the nineteenth century, the Christian element in the situation may not have lost its significance. Klaus Klostermaier notes, somewhat in the spirit of P. J. Marshall, that 'Indologists of that time had to be careful not to challenge the presumed higher age established for the biblical patriarchs.'[52] Thus even the historical rather than legendary dates of biblical figures constituted a kind of glass ceiling which Indian chronology was not supposed to break through.

Developments in the first half of the nineteenth century were extremely influential in shaping western views regarding the sense of history among Hindus. Several of these developments converged to generate the view that the Hindus lacked a sense of history. James Mill, in his highly influential *History of British India*,[53] which appeared in 1817, argued that the Hindus had always been in the condition in which the British now found them. He wrote:

As the manners, institutions, and attainments of the Hindus have been stationary for many ages, in beholding the Hindus of the present day we are beholding the Hindus of many ages past, and are carried back, as it were, into the deepest recesses of antiquity. Nor is this all ... By conversing with the Hindus of the present day, we, in some measure, converse with the Chaldeans and Babylonians of the time of Cyrus: with the Persians and Egyptians of the time of Alexander.[54]

In this sense, then, Hindus had no history, much less a sense for it. Around this time, Hegel (1770–1831) was delivering his highly influential lectures on the philosophy of religion. He concluded on the basis of the material accessible to him that Indian philosophy was static and subtantialist in nature. By calling it static he meant that it lacked 'the dynamics of progress' which characterized Western thought with its origin in Greece. By calling it substantialist, he meant that it espoused the principle of 'substiantiality' (*Substantialität*) or was concerned with the unity and ultimacy of one underlying 'substance'.[55]

There is, in short, a lack of dialectical mediation: The absolute and infinite is not put to work in and for the finite and the relative; and the relative and the finite does not affect the infinite. Accordingly, there is no historical progress towards the enhancement of man and the world.[56]

However, while on the one hand, European scholarship was denying any historical development in India; on the other, European scholars were busy reconstructing its history, a process in which the decipherment of Brāhmī by James Prinsep in 1837 was a major milestone. In the meantime Alexander Cunningham had already embarked on his career in 1831, which would earn him the title of 'father of Indian archaeology'. The absence of a sense of history among the Hindus was further confirmed by the fact that it was the Europeans who were actively engaged in recovering and retrieving it.

Around this time the philological developments, set in motion by William Jones' far reaching suggestion that the languages spoken in India and Europe may have a common ancestor, began to make their impact. They led to the formulation of the celebrated Indo-European hypothesis. According to this hypothesis, the linguistic affinity among the languages spoken in north and north-western parts of the Indian sub-continent and those in parts of Europe is so strong that it can only be explained on the basis of their having sprung from a common tongue. Although the determination of the Indo-European homeland where their common tongue was spoken remains elusive, scholarly opinion soon decisively swung in favour of the view that it lay outside India, with the important historical implication that the Aryans had originally entered India from a point beyond India.

Around the middle of the nineteenth century the suggestion was mooted that the Śūdras of the Hindu caste system might represent the original inhabitants of India, who were reduced to that status by the invading Aryans. Now a coherent picture of events in remote history began to take shape.[57] Once again its effect was to reinforce the view that Hindus lacked a sense of history, because they had lacked awareness of these facts for centuries and their literature did not preserve its memory. One must note here that the evidence of the Indo-European incursion into India is linguistic rather than literary.[58] The absence of such literary evidence further served to confirm the assumption of a lack of sense of history. By the second half of the nineteenth century, the high noon of the British empire witnessed the establishment of the absence of a sense of history of the Hindus as a firm conclusion, almost enjoying the status of an axiom. Moreover, by now the 'Sacred Books' of India had been published in large numbers, and the works on history among Hindus were conspicuous by their absence. This further confirmed the Indologists in their view that Hindus lacked a sense of history. It began to be felt that:

> The weakest spot in the whole domain of Hindu writing, in both Vedic and post-Vedic periods, lies in the province of history. Qualified students almost without exception have held this view. 'The whole course of Sanskrit literature', says Macdonell, 'is darkened by the shadow of this defect.'[59]

A. A. Macdonell deserves to be cited in full here on account of the influential nature of his book, which first appeared in 1900 and is still in print.

> History is the one weak spot in Indian Literature. It is, in fact, non-existent. The total lack of the historical sense is so characteristic that the whole course of Sanskrit literature is darkened by the shadow of this defect, suffering as it does from an entire absence of exact chronology. So true is this, that the very date of KĀLIDĀSA, the

greatest Indian poet, was long a matter of controversy within the limits of a thousand years, and is even now doubtful to the extent of a century or two. Thus the dates of Sanskrit authors are in the vast majority of cases only known approximately, having been inferred from the indirect evidence of interdependence, quotation or allusion, development of language or style. As to the events of their lives, we usually know nothing at all, and only in a few cases one or two general facts. Two causes seem to have combined to bring about this remarkable result. In the first place, early India wrote no history because it never made any. The ancient Indians never went through a struggle for life, like the Greeks in the Persian and the Romans in the Punic wars, such as would have welded their tribes into a nation and developed political greatness. Secondly, the Brahmans, whose task it would naturally have been to record great deeds, had early embraced the doctrine that all action and existence are a positive evil, and could therefore have felt but little inclination to chronicle historical events.[60]

Two other developments did much to magnify the impression that the Hindus lacked a sense of history to the point of utter disregard of it. One of these consisted of allegations and forgery on the part of the priestly class. Benjamin Walker remarks:

The full story of forged texts in Hinduism has yet to be written. It would make a decided contribution to the lengthy chronicle of misplaced piety the world over. The *purusha-sūkta* is only the most conspicuous of a long list of fictitious texts purporting to be genuine. Max Müller has shown how the Brahmins 'mangled, mistranslated and misapplied' the original word *agre* to read *agneḥ* in order to provide *Rig-vedic* support for the burning of widow. As already stated the Epics were drastically overhauled, while the corruption of the Purāṇas and Dharma-śāstras continued till after Muhammadan conquest. Dr. Ambedkar refers to the well-known case in the time of the East India Company, where an entire *smṛiti* was concocted to support a particular lawsuit. And K. M. Panikkar refers to the fabrication of a Śaṅkara text by the Brahmins of Malabār to sanction the inhuman custom of inapproachability.[61]

It is possible to overstate the facts here however. James Mill wrote: 'The Brahmans are the most audacious and perhaps the most unskilful fabricators, with whom the annals of fable have yet made us acquainted.'[62] The charge however received a startling extension at the hands of Dugald Stewart. The following remarks of A. A. Macdonell help explain these developments. He wrote around the turn of the last century:

... till about a hundred and twenty years ago there was no authentic information in Europe about the existence of Sanskrit literature, but only vague surmise, finding expression in stories about the wisdom of the Indians. The enthusiasm with which Voltaire in his *Essai sure les Moeurs et l'Esprit des Nations* greeted the lore of the

Ezour Vedam, a work brought from India and introduced to his notice in the middle of the last century, was premature. For this work was later proved to be a forgery made in the seventeenth century by a Jesuit missionary. The scepticism justified by this fabrication, and indulged in when the discovery of the genuine Sanskrit literature was announced, survived far into the present century.

Thus, Dugald Stewart, the philosopher, wrote an essay in which he endeavoured to prove that not only Sanskrit literature, but also the Sanskrit language, was a forgery made by the crafty Brahmans on the model of Greek after Alexander's conquest. Indeed, this point was elaborately defended by a professor at Dublin as late as the year 1838.[63]

The other development was the increasing identification of Hinduism with Brahmanism. The Brahmanas, as the custodians of the sacred Sanskrit literature of India, were said to be especially indifferent to history. Pargiter, for instance, claimed that, 'The lack of a historical sense was a special characteristic of the Brahmins.'[64] The most severe indictment in that regard is offered by a modern Marxist Brahmin, D. D. Kosambi, who writes:

The brahmin never troubled to record and publish the caste laws he defended. The basis for a broad, general common law on the principles of equality or like the Roman *ius gentium* was lost; crime and sin stand hopelessly confused, while juristic principles are drowned in an amazing mass of religious fable which offers ridiculous justification for any stupid observance. The various guild and city records that existed through the middle ages were never thought worthy of study and analysis. Indian culture lost the contributions that these numerous groups (tribal, clan, *jāti* caste, guild, and perhaps civic) could have made. The civilising and socialising work of the Buddha and of Aśoka was never continued. The tightening of caste bonds and of caste exclusiveness threw away the possibility of finding some common denominator of justice and equity for all men regardless of class, profession, caste, and creed.[65]

He goes on to say:

As a concomitant, almost all-Indian history is also obliterated. The fifth-century tribes (Licchavi, Kallas, and the Aryans in the Punjāb) defended their liberties as stubbornly as any Greek city-state and far more vigorously than Athens again Macedon. Only, no brahmin Aristotle ever studied their constitutions. Their *sabhā* councils saw eloquence (as we know from tradition) comparable to the Athenian in public meetings, but no historian tells us how and what free institutions were destroyed along with the free people. The actual difference between Greek and Indian antiquity was less than appears from comparison of the superb literary quality of the Greek classics with the endless insipid drivel of medieval Sanskrit Purānas. Megasthenes recognised 'free cities' in India, a term with clear historical meaning for the Greeks even when they had been subjugated by Macedon. Aristotle specially notes the common table at Sparta, Crete, and many other Greek cities as an important democratic institution. This is precisely the Yajurvedic *sagdhi* and *sapiti*, eating and drinking in common for which the eighth century Aryan prayed. It is also the decaying institution, *ekapātram* which the eleventh book of the *Arthaśāstra* would use to subvert the freedom of the great Indian oligarchies. It now remains only as a caste taboo on strange food.[66]

Greek and Roman religion required fishing about in the reeking entrails of freshly slaughtered beasts before every important action, for centuries after such customs had gone out of Indian fashion; Themistokles sacrificed human victims on the eve of Salamis. Thus, brahmin indifference to past and present reality not only erased Indian history but a great deal of real Indian culture as well. The loss may be estimated by imagining the works of Aristotle, Herodotus, Thukydides and their contemporaries as replaced by priestly ritual rewritten for the medieval *Patrologia Latina* of Migne, supplemented by excerpts from the *Gesta Romanorum*.[67]

In retrospect there is a certain irony in this. The various manuscripts on the basis of which it could be claimed that there is *some* evidence to support a sense of history among the Hindus were also identified during the latter half of the nineteenth century. Bühler identified the manuscripts of the *Gaudavaho* of Vākpatirāja, which deals with the historical exploits of Yaśovarman (eighth century) and of the *Vikramāṅkadevacarita* of Bilhana, which deals with similar exploits of the Cālukya King Vikramāditya VI (twelfth century) in the Jaina library in Jaisalmer in 1874, while Stern's translation of the *Rājataraṅgiṇī* appeared in 1900.[68]

The first decade of the twentieth century witnessed the identification of the Indus Valley Civilization, with the successful excavations at Harappa in Punjab and Mohanjo-Daro in Sind. These discoveries enabled the current framework of Indian history to be put in place, marking the passage from pre-history to history.

It is clear then that the Hindus could be said to lack a sense of history in several senses. To the extent that written records signal the passage from pre-history to history, the Hindus were latecomers on the scene. When and how writing became known in India is still disputed. Moreover, even in terms of oral transmission, their efforts were directed towards the preservation of their religious literature, the most sacred parts of it were said to be timeless. Even when secular literature did evolve, history was at least neglected. Such historical records as were preserved were preserved haphazardly. And when literary treatment of historical themes was accepted as a legitimate genre it took the form of historical romance rather than historiography.

V

Another factor, which contributed to the notion that the Hindus lacked a sense of history, one may dub as the Heisenberg Principle in Indology. The name of German physicist Heisenberg is associated with the enunciation of a principle of modern physics, which, among other things, 'emphasizes the active role of the scientist, who, in the act of making measurements, interacts with the observed object'.[69] Somewhat comparable phenomena occurred in a few cases when enthusiastic British scholars and civil servants turned avidly to the reconstruction of India's past through a study of its ancient texts.[70] Apparently in some cases their enthusiasm for the collection of these texts itself lead to the appearance of these texts; the active role they played in the collection of manuscripts influenced the availability of these manuscripts, at least arguably in the following two cases.[71]

The first case relates to a text called the *Śukranīti*, a text at one time generally 'utilized as a source for the early medieval period, especially the eleventh or the twelfth century'.[72] In keeping with this practice, however, when Bhakat Prasad Mazumdar utilized this text as a source in his book *The Socio-Economic History of Northern India (11th and 12th centuries)*, K. A. Nilakanta Sastri pointed out in his review of that book: 'opinion is gaining ground of late that the *Śukranītisāra* is really not a work of any considerable antiquity'.[73] Scholarly opinion had been drawn in this direction by the remarks made by Professor V. Raghavan[74] and, taking the cue from him,[75] the Nātiśāstra of Śukra has 'now been shown with practical certainty to be a work of the early nineteenth century.'[76] Lallanji Gopal writes:

> The striking parallelism between our text and the East India Company Regulations of the first quarter of the nineteenth century would suggest that it was composed towards the first half of the century. A study of the existing manuscripts of the texts yields an upper limit for its date. All the dated manuscripts belong to the third quarter of the century, two of the earliest, from the Oriental Institute, Baroda, and the Government Oriental Manuscript's Library, Madras, being respectively dated 1851 and 1852.[77]

What motive underlay the composition of this work? Lallanji Gopal has suggested two main motives; while admitting that 'it is difficult to speak of the motives which actuated the modern writer of *Śukranīti*', he proposed that the author

> may have aimed at pleasing a liberal Sahib who was interested in unearthing lost Sanskrit texts. By presenting a polity in conformity with the practices of the East

India Company he may have wanted to earn the good will of his officers, or else in a patriotic spirit wished to trace some of the details of the administrative machinery of the East India Company back to ancient India.[78]

At another point he suggests:

another possible motive for the production of such a work. It is well known that the East India Company often took charge of the administration of the subordinate rulers on the pretext that they were not efficient and just. It might be that some such Indian ruler, by combining something of the East India Company's administration with ancient Indian practices, wished to convey the impression that his government was based on just and sound principles.[79]

It is clear, therefore, that in either case the motive probably had something to do with pleasing the British sahib. Thus the appearance of the manuscript is in any case connected with the coming of the British—and, what is more, it may even have been directly the result of British interest in Indian antiquities. This is the view of Professor V. Raghavan,[80] who is supported by Professor K. A. Nilakanta Sastri. At no less than two places Professor Sastri associates the production of this work with Col. Mackenzie—at one place indirectly[81] and at the other quite directly, when he states that 'the *Śukranītisāra* is now suspected to be an early nineteenth century hoax calculated to satisfy the comprehensive curiosity of Col. Mackenzie.'[82]

The second case relates to the Purāṇas. It is a popular belief in many circles that information based on the Purāṇas was instrumental, or at least helpful, in determining the source of the Nile, so much so that in spite of criticism about the historical value of the Purāṇas 'the confirmation of the Purāṇic statement as to the source of the Nile by actual discovery by Capt. Speke in Nubia (Kuśadvīpa) turned the tide in favour of the Purāṇas for a while'.[83] Professor D. D. Kosambi supplies even more details when he recounts that 'when J. H. Speke first discovered the *Purāṇas*' with the help of Lieutenant Wilford of Bombay they 'turned out to represent the inner African local names with startling accuracy.'[84]

In his review of the book in which this statement occurs, Professor D. H. H. Ingalls pointed out that this popular view is misleading.

The actual facts deserve mention. Francis Wilford was one of the first European Sanskritists. His study of Sanskrit was prompted in large part by his desire to secure corroboration of Biblical history from Indian tradition. Among his methods of pursuing this end was to recite stories from the Old Testament to a certain pandit, asking this pandit if similar stories could be found in Sanskrit. The pandit duly 'discovered' a circumstantial account of Noah in the *Padmapurāṇa* and an account of Egypt and the Nile in the *Skandapurāṇa*. As for the story of Noah, the pandit seems to have composed it himself, copied it down and inserted it into a *Padmapurāṇa* MS. With the account of Egypt his method was simpler, being to erase geographical names in *Skandapurāṇa* MS and write in their place *miśradeśa* (Arabic *miśr* = Egypt) or *guptadeśa* (*gupta* was taken by Wilford as = Aiguptos). Wilford published a long article on the Puranic accounts of Egypt in *Asiatick Researches* in 1805. Half a century later the explorer Speke was given a copy of Wilford's map. Unaware of Wilford's apology and supposing that all of this cartographic information derived from Indian sources, Speke was easily misled into imputing a particular knowledge of Africa to the ancient Hindus.[85]

It is clear therefore, that Western participation in Indian historiography by itself influenced the historical material on which this historiography is based. However, the critical nature of the historical method is such that in course of time this 'influence' itself was identified and its results detected. But it also raises the further question: is it possible that some elements in modern Indian historiography, which are taken for granted as facts, may be the product of Western Christian enthusiasms for historical documents and Indian responsiveness in satisfying it unbeknownst to us? It is thus useful to bear in mind that the Heisenberg principle also applies to Indology and should put Indologists on guard against being too-certain about some 'facts'.[86]

VI

The issue of the possession of a sense of history, or absence thereof, also figured in the debate between the Orientalists and the Anglicists during the 1830s. Around this time the linguistic medium through which education should be imparted under British rule became a matter of public debate, when the disbursement of public funds for such purposes became a British responsibility. In this debate Lord Macaulay played a crucial role to tilt the scale in favour of English. In his famous *Minute on Education* (1835) the absence of a sense of history on the part of the Hindus was used, in part, to justify the introduction of Western education through English. Lord Macaulay was generally dismissive of the Orientalist position. According to the historians Thompson and Garratt: 'he was profoundly ignorant of the other case (always an advantage, joined to decisiveness such as his).'[87]

Lord Macaulay himself wrote in the Minute:

I am quite ready to take the Oriental learning at the valuation of the Orientalists themselves. I have never found one among them who could deny that a single shelf of a good European library was worth the whole native literature of India and Arabia.[88]

That the lack of a sense of history contributed to his poor assessment is apparent from a perusal of the following passages:

... when we pass from works of imagination to works in which facts are recorded and general principles investigated the superiority of the Europeans become absolutely immeasurable. *It is, I believe, no exaggeration to say that all the historical information which has been collected from all the books written in Sanskrit language is less valuable than what may be found in the most paltry abridgments used at preparatory schools in England* ...

The question now before us is simply whether, when it is in our power to teach this language, we shall teach languages in which by universal confession there are no books on any subject which deserve to be compared to our own; whether, when we can teach European science, we shall teach systems which by universal confession whenever they differ from those of Europe differ for the worse; and whether, when we can patronise sound philosophy and *true history*, we shall countenance at the public expense medical doctrines which would disgrace an English farrier, astronomy which would move laughter in girls at an English boarding school, history abounding with kings thirty feet high and reigns 30,000 years long, and geography made up of seas of treacle and seas of butter ...

It is confessed that a language is barren of useful knowledge. We are to teach it because it is fruitful of monstrous superstitions. We are to teach *false history*, false astronomy, false medicine, because we find them in company with false religion.[89]

So when English became the official language of British India on 7 March 1835, it was at least in part because Sanskrit literature was thought to contain false history.

VII

The rise of the nationalist movement in India, in response to British imperialism, enables one to identify another dimension of the question. This has to do with the absence of a *fair* sense of history. Jawaharlal Nehru, the first prime minister of independent India and himself a historian of some merit, observed:

Very probably all the early records we have of the Aryans in India, their epics and traditions, glorify the Aryans and are unfair to the people of the country whom they subdued. No individual can wholly rid himself of his racial outlook and cultural limitations, and when there is conflict between races and countries even an attempt at impartiality is considered a betrayal of one's own people. War, which is an extreme example of this conflict, results in a deliberate throwing overboard of all fairness and impartiality so far as the enemy nation is concerned; the mind coarsens and becomes closed to almost all avenues of approach except one. The overpowering need of the moment is to justify one's own actions and condemn and blacken those of the enemy. Truth hides somewhere at the bottom of the deepest well, and falsehood, naked and unashamed, reigns almost supreme.[90]

The following passage reflects a mind caught in the passion of the Independence struggle trying to come to grips with the fact that historiography must aim at being not only dispassionate but also fair.

Recent Indian history—that is, the history of the British period—is so connected with present-day happenings that the passions and prejudices of today powerfully influence our interpretation of it. Englishmen and Indians are both likely to err, though their errors will lie in opposite directions. Far the greater part of the records and papers out of which history takes shape and is written come from British sources and inevitably represents the British point of view. The very circumstances of defeat and disruption prevented the Indian side of the story from being properly recorded, and many of the records that existed suffered destruction during the great revolt of 1857. The papers that survived were hidden away in family archives and could not be published for fear of consequences. They remained dispersed, little known, and many perished in the manuscript stage from the incursions of termites and other insects, which abound in this country. At a later stage when some of these papers were discovered, they threw a new light on many historical incidents. Even British-written history had to be somewhat modified, and the Indian conception often very different from the British took shape. Behind this conception lay also a mass of tradition and memories, not of the remote past but of a period when our grandfathers and great-grandfathers were living witnesses, and often the victims, of events. As history this tradition may have little value, but it is important as it enables us to understand the background of the Indian mind today. The villain of the British in India is often a hero to Indians, and those whom the British have delighted to honour and reward are often traitors and Quislings in the eyes of the great majority of the Indian people. That taint clings to their descendants.

It is significant that the cry is not for an 'objective' but 'fair' account. Perhaps Nehru was too much of a Marxist to believe in an 'objective' history; just as he was too much of a nationalist to place his trust in an 'impartial' account either. He goes on to say:

The history of the American Revolution has been differently written by Englishmen and Americans, and even today when old passions have subsided and there is friendship between the two peoples, each version is resented by the other party. In our own day Lenin was a monster and a brigand to many English statesmen of high repute; yet millions have considered him as a saviour and the greatest man of the age. These comparisons will give us some faint idea of the resentment felt by Indians at being forced to study in their schools and colleges so-called histories which disparage India's past in every way, vilify those whose memory they cherish and honour, and glorify the achievements of British rule in India.[91]

Can what is written as history be divorced from who writes it?

END NOTES

1. P. T. Raju, *The Philosophical Traditions of India* (London: George Allen & Unwin Ltd., 1971), p. 15; David R. Kinsley, *Hinduism* (Englewood Cliffs, NJ: Prentice-Hall Inc., 1982), pp. 23–4; Bardwell L. Smith, ed., *The Two Wheels of Dhamma* (AAR Studies in Religion No. 3, 1972), p. 81; N. Subramaniam, *The Hindu Tripod and Other Essays* (Madurai: Koodal Publishers, 1976), p. 118 fn. 27; P. N. Srinivasachari, *The Philosophy of Viśiṣṭādvaita* (Adyar: The Adyar Library and Research Centre, 1970), pp. 180–1; Prabhakar Machwe, *Hinduism* (New Delhi: Vikas Publishing House Pvt. Ltd., 1979), pp. 57–9; Satischandra Chatterjee and Dhirendramohan Datta, *An Introduction to Indian Philosophy* (Calcutta: University of Calcutta, 1968), p. 9; Malcolm Pitt, *Introducing Hinduism* (New York: Friendship Press, 1958), p. 20; Charles F. Keyes and E. Valentine Daniel, eds, *Karma: An Anthropological Inquiry* (Berkeley: University of California Press, 1983), p. 8; G. A. Feurestein, *Introduction to the Bhagavadgītā* (London: Rider & Company, 1974), pp. 28, 36, 41; D. K. Ganguly, *History and Historians in Ancient India* (New Delhi: Abhinav Publications, 1984) Chapter 1, passim; specially pp. 4–7; Charles A. Moore, ed., *The Indian Mind* (Honolulu: East-West Centre, 1967), p. 254; Ainslie T. Embree, ed., *The Hindu Tradition* (New York: Random House, 1966), pp. 208, 220, 251; P. V. Kane, *History of Dharmaśāstra* (Poona: Bhandarkar Oriental Research Institute, 1974) Vol. II, Pt. I, pp. 15, 383, 611 note 15; Vol. III, p. 308; Swami Chidavilasnanda, *Facets of Brahman or the Hindu Gods* (Tirupparaitturai: Tapovanam Printing School, 1971), p. 14 (citing D. S. Sarma); Louis Renou, *Religions of Ancient India* (London: University of Athlone Press, 1953), pp. 46, 50, 51, 75, 89, 92, 94, 123; Sheldon Pollock, 'Mīmāṁsā and the Problem of History in Traditional India,' *Journal of the American Oriental Society* 109:4:603–10 (October–December 1989); Edward Conze, *A Short History of Buddhism* (Bombay: Chetana, 1960), p. xi; M. Hiriyanna, *Outlines of Indian Philosophy* (London: George Allen & Unwin Ltd., 1932), pp. 268–8, 273; Alexander Lipski, *Life and Teachings of Sri Anandamayi Ma* (Delhi: Motilal Banarsidass, 1977), pp. 28–9; Margaret Chatterjee, *Gandhi's Religious Thought* (London: Macmillan Press, 1983), pp. 6–7; D. Mackenzie Brown, *Indian Political Thought From Ranade to Bhave* (Berkeley: University of California Press, 1961), p. 41; A. C. Bouquet, *Hinduism* (London: Hutchinson University Library, 1962), p. 15; S. P. Gupta, ed., K. A. Nilakanta Sastri, *Aspects of India's History and Culture* (Delhi: Oriental Publishers, 1974), p. 13; Heinrich Zimmer, *Myths and Symbols in Indian Art and Civilization* (edited by Joseph Campbell. New York & Evanston:

Harper & Row, 1962), pp. 194–5; Barbara Crosette, *India: Facing the Twenty-First Century* (Bloomington: Indiana University Press, 1993), passim; William Cenkner, *A Tradition of Teachers: Śaṅkara and the Jagadgurus Today* (Delhi: Motilal Banarsidass, 1983), pp. 109–10, 185; S. Radhakrishnan, *Eastern Religions and Western Thought* (Oxford: Clarendon Press, 1939), pp. 128–9, 328; Troy Wilson Organ, *The Hindu Quest for Perfection in Man* (Athens, Ohio: Ohio University, 1970), p. 323; Eric J. Sharpe, *Comparative Religion: A History* (London: Duckworth, 1986), p. 24; Nalinaksha Dutt, *Buddhist Sects in India* (Calcutta: Firma K. L. Mukhopadhay, 1970), p. 62; Frank Whaling, ed., *Contemporary Approaches to the Study of Religion* (Amsterdam: Mouton Publishers, 1984) Vol. I, pp. 216, 218; Vol. II, p. 247; Leonard Swidler, ed., *Toward A Universal Theology of Religion* (Maryknoll, NY: Orbis Books, 1987), pp. 60, 82–3; Joel Larus, *Culture and Political Military Behaviour: The Hindus in Pre-Modern India* (Calcutta: Minerva Associates, 1979), pp. 9–11; Jonathan Z. Smith, *Imagining Religion: From Babylon to Jonestown* (Chicago: University of Chicago Press, 1982), p. 29; Troy Wilson Organ, *Hinduism: Its Historical Development* (Woodbury, NY: Barron's Educational Series, 1974), pp. 4–9; Klaus K. Klostermaier, *A Survey of Hinduism* (second edition) (Albany, NY: State University of New York Press, 1989), pp. 81; K. Satchidananda Murty, *Revelation and Reason in Advaita Vedānta* (Delhi: Motilal Banarsidass, 1974), p. 217; Heinrich von Stietencron, 'Political Aspects of Indian Religious Art', *Visible Religion* Vol. IV/V (Brill: Leiden, 1985/6), p. 16; A. L. Basham, 'Medieval Hindu India,' in A. L. Basham, ed., *A Cultural History of India* (Delhi: Oxford University Press, 1975), p. 54 where he speaks of 'no real historical tradition' in India; Huston Smith, 'Wasson's Soma: A Review Article,' *Journal of the American Academy of Religion* Vol. XL:4:481 (December 1972) where he refers to 'characteristic Indian casualness toward history;' A. Berriedale Keith, *A History of Sanskrit Literature* (London: Oxford University Press, 1920), pp. 144–7; R. C. Zaehner, ed., *The Concise Encyclopedia of Living Faiths* (Boston: Beacon Press, 1959), p. 20: Zaehner refers to Indian religions as 'anything but historically-minded'; J. W. McCrindle, *Ancient India as Described by Megasthenes and Arrian* (Calcutta: Chuckervertty, Chatterjee and Co. Ltd., 1960), p. 10, footnote which contains the statement: 'when even the Indian historians have no authority in history ... '; Jawaharlal Nehru, *The Discovery of India* (New York: The John Day Company, 1946), pp. 92–5; M. Winternitz, *A History of Indian Literature* (Calcutta: University of Calcutta, 1927) Vol. I, p. 29; H. G. Rawlinson, *Intercourse Between India and the Western World From the Earliest Times to the Fall of Rome* (second edition) (New York: Octagon Books, 1971 [1916]), p. 60. Kenneth S. Ch'en, *Buddhism: The Light of Asia* (Hauppage, New York: Barron's Educational Series Inc., 1968), pp. 1–2; D. D. Kosambi, *The Culture and Civilisation of Ancient India in Historical Outline* (Delhi, Bombay, Bangalore: Vikas Publications, 1970), pp. 173–4; James Mill, *The History of British India* (abridged and with an introduction by William Thomas) (Chicago and London: The University of Chicago Press, 1975), p. 36: 'We have perhaps but little to regret the total absence of Hindu records'; Prakash N. Desai, *Health and Medicine in the Hindu Tradition: Continuity and Cohesion* (New York: Crossroads, 1989), p. 9: 'A tradition of assigning specific dates is absent in early India ... '; Amaury de Riencourt, *The Soul of India* (New Delhi: Stirling Publishers Private Limited, 1960), p. xii, 9; Gavin Flood, *An Introduction to Hinduism* (Cambridge: Cambridge University Press, 1996), pp. 20–1; E. J. Rapson, 'Sources of History,' in E. J. Rapson, *Ancient India* (Cambridge: Cambridge University Press, 1922), pp. 57–9, Romila Thapar, *Ancient Indian Social History: Some Interpretations* (New Delhi: Orient Longman, 1978), p. 1, alludes to the 'stereotypes of "unchanging India" and her "unhistorical" religions and peoples', also see p. 268; Ashis Nandy, *Alternative Sciences: Creativity and Authenticity in Two Indian Scientists* (New Delhi: Allied Publishers Private Limited, 1980), p. 4, where he describes himself as 'brought up on the orientalist belief that Indian culture was ahistorical;' U. N. Ghosal, *Studies in Indian History and Culture* (Bombay: Orient Longmans, 1965), p. 1; etc.

2. A. L. Basham, *The Wonder that was India* (third revised edition) (New Delhi: Rupa & Co., 1999 [1954]), p. 44.

3. Ibid., p. 4.

4. Klaus K. Klostermaier, *A Survey of Hinduism* (second edition) (Albany, NY: State University of New York Press, 1994), p. 117.

5. Malcolm Pitt, op. cit., p. 20.

6. J. W. McCrindle, op. cit., p. 109; S. Krishnaswami Aiyangar, *Ancient India and South Indian History & Culture* (Poona: Oriental Book Agency, 1941), Vol. I, p. 145: 'India has had some episodes but no history' (Henri Barr, cited in Stuart Piggott, *Prehistoric India to 1000* BC [Harmondsworth: Penguin, 1950], p. 11). Some have interestingly argued that far from having no history, India may had enough of it like China, see Amaury de Riencourt, op. cit., pp. xi, xii. But for James Mill: 'Their annals, however, from that [Alexander's] era till the period of the Mahomedan conquests, are a blank.' (op. cit., p. 35).

7. Sometimes the lack of a sense of chronology is also included (U. N. Ghosal, op. cit., p. 27, note 29); S. Krishnaswami Aiyangar, op. cit., Vol. I, p. 416. Romila Thapar offers the following useful statement on how the expression 'a sense of history' might be understood in the present context (op. cit., pp. 268–9): 'Since much of the argument hinges on the definition of a sense of history, let me begin by suggesting a definition. A sense of history can be defined as a consciousness of past events, which events are relevant to a particular society, seen in a chronological framework and expressed in a form which meets the needs of that society. It may be argued that this is too restricted a definition and that history implies a concern with political events and, in addition, involves the analysis of past events by suggesting causal relationships based on rational explanation and which, therefore, assumes a critical judgement on the past by the historian. It is, however, debatable whether this extension of the definition of an historical sense is not a product of modern thinking, and where such historical writing does exist in ancient cultures (as indeed it does even in the Indian tradition at a later period), it is not a consciously though-out philosophy of history but the result of an individual and rather analytical mind applying itself to historical narrative.'

8. U. N. Ghosal, op. cit., p.1.; R. C. Majumdar, *Ancient India* (New Delhi: Motilal Banarsidass, 1964), p. 7.

9. Pratima Asthana, *The Indian View of History* (Agra: M.G. Publishers, 1992), p. 20.

10. A. L. Basham, *op, cit.*, p. 44. Elsewhere A. L. Basham clearly states: 'All evidence would show that Buddhism had a stronger sense of history than had Hinduism' (A. L. Basham, *Studies in Indian History and Culture* [Calcutta: Sambodhi Publications Private Ltd., 1964], p. 46); A. Beriedale Keith also seems to be inclined towards a similar view, op. cit., p. 148. That a Tibetan Buddhist, Tārānātha, wrote a famous 'History of Buddhism in India' in the sixteenth/seventeenth century seems to confirm this, see P. V. Bapat, ed., *2500 Years of Buddhism* (New Delhi: The Publications Division, Government of India, 1959), p. 173.

11. Padmanabh S. Jaini, *The Jaina Path of Purification* (Berkeley: University of California Press, 1979), pp. 37–8.

12. See Khuswant Singh, *A History of the Sikhs* (Princeton, NJ: Princeton University Press, 1966) 2 vols; Einslie T. Embree, ed., *Sources of Indian Tradition* (second edition) (New York: Columbia University Press, 1988) Vol. I, p. 493.

13. W. Owen Cole and Piara Singh Sambhi, *The Sikhs: Their Religious Beliefs and Practices* (second fully revised edition) (Portland, Oregon: Sussex Academic Press, 1998), p. 8: 'History is important to the Sikh in a way it is not to the Hindu, Buddhist or Jain'; Nirmal Kumar Jain, *Sikh Religion and Philosophy* (New Delhi: Sterling Publishers Pvt Ltd., 1979), p. 94: 'The Gurus have not shown any contempt for history. In this they have not agreed with the Indian tradition. Guru Gobind Singh went to the extent of writing contemporary history himself. Among the last pieces of advice Guru Gobind Singh gave to his disciples one was: "Read the history of your gurus from the time of Guru Nanak".'

14. R. C. Collingwood, cited in D. K. Ganguly, op. cit., p. 31, note 11.

15. R. C. Majumdar, *The Classical Accounts of India* (Calcutta: Firma K. L. Mukhopadhyay, 1960); H. G. Rawlinson, op. cit., passim.

16. For the Greek text see E. A. Schwanbeck, ed., *Megasthenes Indica* (Amsterdam: Verlag Adolf M. Harkert, 1966); for translation see J. W. McCrindle, op. cit.

17. Ramchandra Jain, ed., *McCrindle's Ancient India as Described by Megasthenes and Arrian* (New Delhi: Today & Tomorrow's Printers & Publishers, 1972), p. 107–08, emphasis added. For an attempt to connect this account with traditional Indian accounts see Shankar Goyal, *History of Writing of Early India: New Discoveries and Approaches* (Jodhpur: Kusamanjali Prakashan, 1996), p. 10: '[I]n this connection the first point of great significance is that while discussing Heracles with reference to Mathurā, Megasthenes confuses or identifies him with Manu Vaivasvata also and places him 138 generations before Sandracottus (Chandragupta). Now, according to the genealogical tables of the Paurāṇic dynasties prepared by Pargiter, from Manu to the fall of the Nandas 135 generations had ruled over the various parts of the country: Chandragupta Maurya himself belonged to the 136th generation. The significance of this fact from the point of view of the state of the Paurāṇic literature in the age of Megasthenes is that it proves, rather conclusively, that whatever the condition of the detailed myths and legends associated with the various kings, at least the genealogical lists, available in the days of Megasthenes were not much different

from the lists as found in the present-day Purāṇas. The importance of this conclusion for the history of the Vedic age can hardly be over-emphasized.'

18. H. G. Rawlinson, op. cit., p. 60.

19. Ibid., p. 115.

20. R. C. Majumdar, *The Classical Accounts of India*, p. 223.

21. 'It is not known from what sources Megasthenes derived these figures, which are extremely modest when compared with those of Indian chronology, where, as in geology, years are hardly reckoned but in myriads' (J. W. McCrindle, op. cit., p. 208).

22. P. V. Kane, op. cit., Vol. II, p. 901.

23. A. L. Basham, op. cit., p. 58.

24. Ibid., p. 493. On these eras see ibid., Appendix III; Ainslie T. Embree, ed., *Alberuni's India Translated by Edward C. Sachau* (abridged edition) (New York: W. W. Norton & Co., Inc., 1971), Chapter XLIX.

25. For an interesting testimony to this fact see J. L. Nehru, op. cit., pp. 93–4.

26. Two further points may be worth noting by way of comparison with Greek culture: (1) the unique lack of Hindu historiography prior to Kalhaṇa has been compared to the uniqueness of Greek monolingualism as a cultural feature. D. K. Ganguly writes (op. cit., p. 8): 'A parallel instance of lack of interest explaining a historical phenomenon may be noticed in the ancient Greeks' predilection for monolingualism and refusal to learn a foreign language. "The Greeks", Arnaldo Momigliano writes, "remained proudly monolingual as, with rare exceptions, they had been for centuries." Whereas the Romans and the Jews mastered Greek, the Greeks did not evince interest in the study of Latin, Hebrew and Aramaic. This is indicative of one's attitude of mind but is seldom a reflection of one's competence'; (2) Greek historiography also contains mythical and speculative elements, like the Hindu counterpart but it also goes beyond it. D. K. Ganguly notes (op. cit., p. 31, note 11): 'This is not to say that legendary elements, theocratic or mythical, are entirely absent from historical works composed in these countries. Even the works of Herodotus and Thucydides are not wholly free from such blemishes. The following citation from R. G. Collingwood (*The Idea of History*, London, 1961, p. 18) is worth considering: "But what is remarkable about the Greeks was not the fact that their historical thought combined a certain residue of elements which we should call non-historical thought but the fact that side by side with these it contained elements of what we call history."'

27. K. S. Ch'en, op. cit., pp. 1–2.

28. D. C. Sircar, *Early Indian Numismatic and Epigraphical Studies* (Calcutta: Indian Museum, 1977), p. 21.

29. Ibid.

30. N. Mahalingam, *Historic Dates* (Madras: International Society for the Investigation of Ancient Civilizations, 1991), pp. 31, 43.

31. K. S. Ch'en, op. cit., p. 158.

32. R. C. Majumdar, ed., *The Age of Imperial Unity* (Bombay: Bharatiya Vidya Bhavan, 1968), p. 36.

33. James Legge, tr., *A Record of Buddhist Kingdoms Being An Account By the*

Chinese Monk Fa-hien of his Travels in India and Ceylon (AD 399–414) in Search of the Buddhist Books of Discipline (New York: Dover Publications Inc., 1965; [1886]), p. 43, emphasis added.

34. Ibid., pp. 98–9.

35. Padmanabh S. Jaini, op. cit., p. 50.

36. D. Devahuti, *Harsha: A Political Study* (Oxford: Clarendon Press, 1970), p. 1.

37. Samuel Beal, *Buddhist Records of the Western World Translated from the Chinese of Hiuen Tsiang (AD 629)* (Delhi: Munshiram Manoharlal, 1969; [1884]), p. 78.

38. Ibid., pp. 215–17.

39. J. Takakusu, tr., *A Record of the Buddhist Religion as Practiced in India and the Malay Archipelago (AD 671–695)* (Delhi: Munshiram Manoharlal, 1966; [1896]), pp. 177–8. The fact that they follow whatever occupation they like possesses a striking parallel in Megasthenes' account (see J.W. McCrindle, op. cit., pp. 85–6).

40. Ibid., pp. 182–3.

41. James Legge, tr., op. cit., pp. 57–8. Also see pp. 99–100: 'In consequence (of this success in his quest) Fa-hien stayed here for three years, learning Sanskrit books and the Sanskrit speech, and writing out the Vinaya rules. When Tao-ching arrived in the Central Kingdom, and saw the rules observed by the Śramaṇas, and the dignified demeanour in their societies which he remarked under all occurring circumstances, he sadly called to mind in what a mutilated and imperfect condition the rules were among the monkish communities in the land of Ts'in, and made the following aspiration: 'From this time forth till I come to the state of Buddha, let me not be born in a frontier land.' He remained accordingly (in India), and did not return (to the land of Han). Fa-hien, however, whose original purpose had been to secure the introduction of the complete Vinaya rules into the land of Han, returned there alone.'

42. J. Takakusu, op. cit., p. 169. Also see Jawaharlal Nehru, op. cit., pp. 190–1.

43. See Hemchandra Raychaudhuri, *Political History of Ancient India, with a Commentary by B.N. Mukherjee* (New Delhi: Oxford University Press, 1999), p. 467.

44. Rama Shankar Tripathi, *History of Ancient India* (Delhi: Motilal Banarsidass, 1967), p. 238.

45. Percival Spear, ed., *The Oxford History of India by the Late Vincent A. Smith, C.I.E.* (fourth edition) (Delhi: Oxford University Press, 1994), p. 16. This is itself an abbreviation of *Kitāb taḥqīq mā lil-Hind min maqbūlah lil-'aql aw mardhūlah* (The Book Confirming What Pertains to India, Whether Rational or Despicable), see Bruce Lawrence 'Biruni, Al- (Ah362–442/973–1051 CE)' in Mircea Eliade, editor in chief, *The Encyclopedia of Religion* (New York: Macmillan Publishing Company, 1987) Vol. II, p. 232.

46. Ainslie T. Embree, ed., *Alberuni's India Translated by Edward C. Sachau* (New York: W.W. Norton & Company, 1971) Part II, pp. 10–11. This passage has become the *locus classicus* of the claim that the Hindus lack a sense of history and is often cited; see Benjamin Walker, *The Hindu World* (New York & Washington: Frederick A. Praeger, 1968) Vol. I, p. 454; Rama Shankar Tripathi, *History of*

Ancient India (Delhi: Motilal Banarsidass, 1967 [1942]), p. 1; U. N. Ghosal, op. cit., p. 1; Maurice Winternitz, op. cit., p. 29; D. K. Ganguly, op. cit., p. 32, note 21.

47. R. C. Majumdar, 'Sources of Indian History' in R. C. Majumdar, ed., *The Vedic Age* (London: George Allen & Unwin Ltd., 1952), p. 53.

48. Shankar Goyal, op. cit., p. 60

49. Ibid., p. 103

50. Ibid., p. 104.

51. P. J. Marshall, ed. *The British Discovery of Hinduism in the Eighteenth Century* (Cambridge: Cambridge University Press, 1970), p. 38.

52. Klaus K. Klostermaler, op. cit., p. 478.

53. Richard H. Davis, Introduction, in Donald S. Lopez, Jr., *Religions of India in Practice* (Princeton, New Jersey: Princeton University Press, 1995), p. 46.

54. Cited in William Thomas, ed. *James Mill: The History of British India* (Chicago and London: The University of Chicago Press, 1975), p. xxvi.

55. Wilhelm Halbfass, *India and Europe: An Essay in Understanding* (Albany, NY: SUNY Press, 1988), p. 88.

56. Ibid., p. 90.

57. Ram Sharan Sharma, *Śūdras in Ancient India* (Delhi: Motilal Banarsidass, 1980), p. 9.

58. John Keay, *India: A History* (New York: Atlantic Monthly Press, 2000), pp. 26–7; Percival Spear, ed. op. cit., p. 53; T. Burrow, 'The Early Aryans', in A. L. Basham, ed., *A Cultural History of India* (Delhi: Oxford University Press, 1975), p. 21.

59. Benjamin Walker, op. cit., Vol. I, p. 453.

60. A. A. Macdonell, *A History of Sanskrit Literature* (London: William Heinemann, 1900), pp. 10–11. In assessing his remarks, however, it must be borne in mind that Kalhaṇa's *Rajataraṅgiṇī* (ibid., p. 430), which had only just appeared, is mentioned in an appendix. Discussing Hindu historiography without Kalhaṇa is like discussing Hindu statecraft without Kauṭilya.

61. Benjamin Walker, op. cit., Vol. I, pp. 364–5. Max Müller may have barked up the wrong tree. Charles Lanman notes regarding ṚgVeda X.18.7 (wherein *agre* occurs): 'From Müller's Essay on Comparative Mythology, Chips, ii. 34f, or *Selected Essays*, Vol. I (ed. of 1881), p. 333f, it would appear that the seventh stanza of our hymn had played a great role in Hindu history. At any rate, this idea is current, and seems traceable to the Essay. Here it is stated that the stanza was purposely falsified by an unscrupulous priesthood, and that a garbled version of it, reading *agneḥ* for *agre*, was directly responsible for the sacrifice of thousands of innocent lives. That the author is in error on these points is argued with great detail by Fitzedward Hall, JRAS. Ns.iii.183–92. He shows that the misreading can be traced to Raghunandana, ca. 1500 AD, and no further; and that Suttee was deemed to be amply justified by warrants other than those of the Vedic Saṁhitā, which was by no means the ultimate appeal for the mediaeval Hindu' (*A Sanskrit Reader* [Cambridge, Massachusetts: Harvard University Press, 1978 (1884)], pp. 382–3).

62. James Mill, op. cit., p. 34.

63. Arthur A. Macdonnell, op. cit., pp. 1–2.

64. Ibid., p. 453.

65. D. D. Kosambi, *The Culture and Civilization of Ancient India in Historical Outline* (New Delhi: Vikas Publications, 1970), p. 173.

66. Ibid., pp. 173–4.

67. Ibid., p. 174.

68. Chandra Prabha, *Historical Mahākāvyas in Sanskrit (Eleventh to Fifteenth century AD)* (New Delhi: Shri Bharat Bharati Pvt. Ltd., 1976), p. 79.

69. See *The New Encyclopedia Britannica* (Chicago: Helen Hemingway Benton, 1974), Vol. 8, p. 746.

70. It is widely acknowledged that the restoration of an account of India's past was the work of Western scholarship, in which the British played a key role. See A. L. Basham, op. cit., pp. 4–8.

71. In terms of macroeconomic theory what we have here is Say's Law operating in reverse: demand creating its own supply.

72. Lallanji Gopal, 'The *Śukranīti*—A Nineteenth Century Text', *Bulletin of the School of Oriental and African Studies*, Vol. XXV: Pt 3, 1962, p. 524.

73. Ibid.

74. Ibid.

75. Ibid.

76. A. L. Basham, op. cit., p. 81.

77. Lallanji Gopal, op. cit., p. 551.

78. Ibid.

79. Ibid., p. 553.

80. Ibid., p. 554.

81. See *Journal of Indian History*, Vol. 39, Pt I, p. 197 (April 1961).

82. K. A. Nilakanta Sastri, *Sources of Indian History with Special Reference to South India* (New York: Asia Publishing House, 1964), p. 28. It is curious that A. L. Basham (op. cit., p. 81 fn.) does not refer to this aspect of the issue at all. Jawaharlal Nehru relies on this source heavily for his depiction of ancient Indian polity (*The Discovery of India* [New York: The John Day Company, 1946] p. 245): 'There is an old book, of the tenth century, which gives us some idea of Indian polity as it was conceived prior to the Turkish and Afghan invasions. This is the *Nitisara*, the *Science of Polity*, by Shukracharya. It deals with the organization of the central government as well as of town and village life; of the King's Council of state and various departments of government. The village panchayat or elected council had large powers, both executive and judicial, and its members were treated with the greatest respect by the king's officers. Land was distributed by this panchayat, which also collected taxes out of the produce and paid the government's share on behalf of the village. Over a number of these village councils there were a larger panchayat or council to supervise and interfere if necessary.

Some old inscriptions further tell us how the members of the village councils were elected and what their qualifications and disqualifications were. Various committees were formed, elected annually, and women could serve on them. In case of misbehavior a member could be removed. A member could be disqualified if he failed to render accounts of public funds. An interesting rule to prevent nepotism is mentioned: near relatives of members were not to be appointed to public office.

These village councils were very jealous of their liberties, and it was laid down that no soldier could enter the village unless he had a royal permit. If the people complained of an official, the *Nitisara* says that the king "should take the side not of his officers but of his subjects". If many complained, then the official was to be dismissed, "for who does not get intoxicated by drinking of the vanity of office?" The king was to act in accordance with the opinion of the majority of the people. "Public opinion is more powerful than the king as the rope made of many fibers is strong enough to drag a lion." "In making official appointments work, character and merit were to be regarded—neither caste nor family," and "neither through colour nor through ancestors can the spirit worthy of a Brahmin be generated."'

83. A. D. Pusalkar, *Studies in the Epics and Purāṇas of India* (Bombay: Bharatiya Vidya Bhavan, 1963), p. 41.

84. Damodar Dharmanand Kosambi, *An Introduction to the Study of Indian History* (Bombay: Popular Book Depot, 1956), p. 230.

85. Ibid., pp. 224–5. The following item of information also belongs here: 'Francis Wilford (c. 1760–1822) had served in the company's engineers, spending the latter part of his life at Banaras. He studied ancient Indian geography and tried to show that the British Isles were mentioned in the *Purāṇas* (M. A. Laird, ed., *Bishop Heber in Northern India: Selections from Heber's Journal* [Cambridge: Cambridge University Press, 1971], p. 223, note 1).

86. The following remarks also illustrate the operation of the Heisenberg principle: 'No sustained attempt was made to place the source material in the context of its contemporary background. The sources, particularly those in Sanskrit, were in the main the works of the brahmans, as keepers of the ancient classical tradition, and expressed the Brahmanical Weltanschauung. The fact that these were texts emanating from and relating to a particular segment of society was often overlooked, though in fairness to the Orientalists it must be said that the critical and analytical study of literature from other classical cultures was still in its infancy. The reliance on "pandits", those learned in Sanskrit and supposedly the guardians of the ancient tradition, was not the most reliable—although undoubtedly the most convenient—access to ancient history. Many of the contemporary ideological prejudices of the pandits were often incorporated into what was believed to be the interpretation of the ancient tradition. This vitiated the study of "ancient culture", particularly the section of it which was concerned with the law-books and legal codes, the *dharma-shastras*.' (Romila Thapar, op. cit., pp. 3–4).

87. Edward Thompson and G. T. Garratt, *Rise and Fulfillment of British Rule in India* (Allahabad: Central Book Depot, 1962), p. 660.

88. Cited, ibid., p. 661.

89. Ibid. Emphasis added.

90. Jawaharlal Nehru, op. cit., p. 291.

91. Ibid., p. 289.

Implications of such a View for Indian Studies

I

The proposition that the Hindus did not possess a sense of history, even after the emergence and wide prevalence of this proposition has been established, might still elicit a yawn from the reader. It might best be treated as a curiosity interesting to know but difficult to attach any further importance to. The German army did not possess the institution of the officer's mess the way the British army did; the Japanese business offices, even when posing a threat to the American business on a worldwide basis, did so without the use of the typewriter; the Chinese, despite their long history and an extended feudal period, never produced a real tradition of epic poetry worth its salt; the ancient Greeks remained proudly and even obstinately monolingual notwithstanding their immense intellectual curiosity—these are all interesting facts to know so far as they go, but how far do they take us? Does not the claim, even when considered well-substantiated, that the Hindus had no sense of history, only rise to the level of curiosity and no further?

Such a view would only be justified if one did not realise how pervasive the influence of this proposition has been in shaping the various facets of Indological study. Some British Governor-General's even held that Hindus were a sub-human species,[1] although we have no evidence that Nietzsche's view that 'only the beast lives unhistorically',[2] led them to this view. But other connections are clearer.

History

If the Hindus did not possess a sense of history then they could hardly be relied upon to provide one either of their country or their civilization. This meant many things. First of all it meant that India's history, such as we possess, must have been written by foreigners. As an Indian, Dhan Gopal Mukherji, puts it:

Properly speaking India has no history. We as a race have no consciousness of it, for our history has been written mostly by foreigners—the Greeks, the Arabs and the Chinese. The consciousness of history as an asset of life and as an expression of people does not seem important to us. History is the record of man's relation to time, but the Hindu does not believe in time, and all our life, according to the Hindu's vision, is an illusion and something to be transcended.[3]

This also implies that *even today* Indians may not be capable of writing their own history, although exposed to modern historiography. Another Indian, Nirad C. Chaudhuri puts it mordantly: 'History conferences in India always remind me of seances.'[4] This point should be distinguished from the fact that the history of India such as we possess today is the work of foreign scholars. As Benjamin Walker notes:

The credit for unravelling the skein of India's hoary ancestry, and the restoration of her ancient heritage goes, in the main, to British scholars. A reinterpretation of the sacred records in which the historical material was embedded, in the light of scientific research, had to await the Europeans. The Hindu tradition, the old legends and ballads were of course known to the people, for these were part of their art, their song, their architecture and painting. But few knew the classics at first hand, or were acquainted with what had gone before. Pride in India's immemorial heritage is only of recent birth, inspired to a great extent by Western scholarship and enthusiasm. Summing up this debt, K. M. Panikkar says, 'Today when we talk of the Mauryas, the Guptas, the Chalukyas and the Pallavas, let it be remembered that these great ages of Indian history were recovered to us by the devoted labours of European scholars.'[5]

Troy Wilson Organ even has a dig at the Indian historian quoted in the above passage, as if to imply that Indians still have a long way to go in intellectually emulating their erstwhile European masters.

K. M. Panikkar's popular little book, *A Survey of Indian History*, published on the day of India's independence from British rule (August 15, 1947), and written according to the author to meet 'a growing demand for history of India which would try and reconstruct the past in a way that would give us an idea of our heritage' contains not one chronological table.[6]

The historiographic complications thus introduced are complex. R. C. Majumdar draws attention to one facet of the issue when he writes:

> The first thing to remember is that for the longest period of Indian history, viz., from the earliest time down to the Muslim conquest in the thirteenth century AD, a period of about four thousand years, we possess no historical text of any kind, much less such a detailed narrative as we possess in the case of Greece, Rome, and China. The history of ancient India resembles, therefore, that of ancient Egypt and Mesopotamia. In all these cases it has only been possible to reconstruct the skeleton with the help of archaeological evidence discovered in comparatively recent times. This history differs radically from what we normally understand by the word.[7]

Yet the fact that Indian history at the same time also differs from those of Egypt and Mesopotamia serves to introduce a further complication:

> The chief difference between India and the other ancient countries mentioned above lies in the continuity of her history and civilization. The culture and civilization of Egypt, Sumer, Akkad, Babylon, Assyria, and Persia have long ceased to exist. They are now mere past memories and their history possesses only an academic interest. Indian history and institutions, however, form an unbroken chain by which the past is indissolubly linked up with the present.
>
> The modern peoples of Egypt and Mesopotamia have no bond whatsoever with the civilization that flourished there millennia ago and its memorials have no more (usually very very much less) meaning to them than to any enlightened man in any part of the world.
>
> But not so in India. The icons discovered at Mohenjo-Daro are those of gods and goddesses who are still worshiped in India, and the Hindus from the Himalaya to Cape Comorin repeat even today the Vedic hymns which were uttered on the banks of the Indus nearly four thousand years ago. This continuity in language and literature, and in religious and social usages, is more prominent in India than even in Greece and Italy, where we can trace the same continuity in history.[8]

This means that:

> In the writing of a cultural history of India the problem of finding a date for the origin of a movement is topped by the problem of fixing a date for the terminus of a movement, for, as has often been said, India is a land where nothing ever dies. The traditional morning prayer of the Hindu has been unchanged for three thousand years; the marriage ceremony is at least two thousand years old; and in Poona there is a school for the training of priests to conduct Vedic sacrifices, even though none has been seriously performed for three thousand years.[9]

It has even been proposed that the Aryan invasion wiped out the preceding history of India. Amaury de Riencourt writes:

With the arrival of the Aryan war bands, all historical evidence vanished; script disappeared, and the wooden structures of the Aryans rotted away in time without leaving any traces. From the very first, the invaders manifested the most remarkable trait of Indian psychology; a complete, instinctive indifference to history and the preservation of historical records. The Aryans in India had no memory. And instead of historical treatises such as the Chinese have left to posterity, the Aryans left us *myths*—the transmutation of *time-bound* historical events into timeless tales in which fact and fancy are almost inextricably mixed. So that we are left with the Aryans' first great literary work, the *Ṛg-Veda*, as the unique source of information for this dark period of India's history—and with the tools of a modern psychoanalyst.[10]

The foregoing analysis carries the further implication that foreign sources may be preferred over indigenous sources as avenues of information about India. This would explain why 'at a certain stage in the course of Vedic studies, the principle of Roth that Sāyaṇa must not be read if one is to understand the Veda became the guiding principle'.[11]

It would also explain why Al-Bīrūnī would be eulogized in the following manner despite the fact that identifiable errors do exist in his justly famous account of India.[12]

Al-Biruni, who was born in Chwarezm in Central Asia in 973 AD and died in Ghazni (in present-day Afghanistan) in 1048 AD, ranks as one of the greatest scholars ever, not only of the Islamic or medieval world of his day. At the time when the Turkish conqueror Mahmud of Ghazni took him along to his court from the conquered Chwarezm, he was already one of the leading astronomers, mathematicians and geographers of his time. He devoted himself to the study of the Indian world from Ghazni. This was obviously in connection with Mahmud's military activities in northern India. However, his own remarks indicate that the compilation of his book on India, which he wrote in Arabic, did not result from a direct order of his ruler. Biruni, who, on the one hand, deplored his lack of freedom, and on the other hand appreciated the favourable external circumstances of his work, referred to a suggestion by Abu Sahl. As he says himself, his goal is, above all, a presentation of the facts, a clear and sober description of a religion and philosophy, which has been entirely unknown or misunderstood so far. His enterprise resulted in a pioneering piece of work, equally innovative with regard to its content and methodology. To be sure, the Indian scene had changed considerably since the days of Megasthenes, the representative Greek 'Indologist', but apart from this, it is Al-Biruni's radically new approach, which is most significant and conspicuous.[13]

POLITICS

The concept of a nation-state is central to modern historical and political discourse. According to H. G. Rawlinson:

This lack of national consciousness is perhaps the main reason why pre-Muhammadan India has no historians. Her vast literature contains no Herodotus or Thucydides, no Tacitus or Livy; the very memory of her greatest ruler, the emperor Asoka, was forgotten, until European scholars at the beginning of the 19th century laboriously reconstructed the story by piecing together the fragments which had survived the ravages of time.[14]

It is worth adding that Rawlinson does ascribe some element of national feeling to the Hindus in the post-Muhammadan period. He cites Bajirao as declaring, after being invested with his father's robes of office in 1720:

'Now is the time, to drive the strangers from the land of the Hindus! Let us strike at the trunk of the withering tree, and the branches will fall off themselves. By directing our efforts to Hindustan, the Maratha flag shall fly from the Kistna to Attock.'[15]

K. M. Panikkar makes a point similar to Rawlinson's when he writes:

Muslim nationalism had a developed historiography behind it; but the Hindus, though they had a considerable historical tradition embodied in the Purāṇas, *Kāvyas* and other forms of literature, had not developed history as a separate branch of knowledge. Nothing was therefore known of Indian history before the advent of the Muslims, which was a major fact, which stood in the way of the emergence of a conception of Hindu nationhood. British historians in the early period accepted the Muslim view of Indian history as may be seen from Elliott and Dawson's strange volumes of the *Chronicles of Islamic Kingdoms* which they style the 'History of India told by her own historians'. Of the two thousand years of Indian history before Islam entered India, the early historians of India know nothing because there was, as we said, no developed Hindu historiography.[16]

The lack of a sense of history produces problems not only for the concept of the 'nation' but also of the 'state'. The concept of the state, as defined by Hegel for instance, requires a sense of agency and scope for dialectical mediation. Both of these are denied by Hegel to Hindu thought, as will be discussed later. And, as for him 'philosophical thought and social and political reality were inseparable',[17] it comes as no surprise that he should conclude: 'Hindu political existence presents us with a people, but *no state*.'[18]

In a curious union of opposites, the political implication of a quiescent or turbulent history both served to negate political agency. V. A. Smith, for instance, takes the latter route. He is cited as follows at the beginning of a chapter entitled: 'Forgotten Episodes in the History of Medieval India' by Krishnaswami Aiyangar:

'Harsha's death must have loosened the bonds, which have restrained the disruptive forces, always ready to operate in India, and led them to produce their natural result, a medley of petty states with very varying boundaries, and engaged in internecine war. Such was India when first disclosed to European observation in the fourth century, and such it always had been except during the comparatively brief periods in which a vigorous central government has compelled the mutually repellent molecules of the body politic to check their gyrations and submit to the grasp of a superior controlling force.' These are the terms in which the talented author of the *Early History of India* described the condition of affairs that followed the death of Harsha. The century following, namely, the period from AD 650 to 750 is comparatively barren of events so far as Hindu India as hitherto known, is concerned.[19]

The concept of Oriental Despotism can also be traced back to this lack of a sense of history, which went hand in hand with the concept of a static society.

Mill's assertion that the Indian past had been that of an unchanging, static society dominated by despotic rulers was reflected in various philosophies of history current in the nineteenth century. The most influential of these with respect to Indian history were the works of Hegel. For Hegel, of course, true history involved dialectical change and development. Indian history remained stationary and fixed and therefore outside the stream of world history. The basis of Indian society was the immutable pattern of the Indian village, inhabited by a people totally unconcerned with political relationships. This permitted not only despotic rulers but also frequent conquests and continual subjugation. The static character of Indian society with its concomitant despotic rulers became an accepted truth of Indian history. The concept of Oriental Despotism began to take shape.[20]

Sociology and Economics

A society without a history is a static society. The application of the proposition of a lack of sense of history to the social arena in the case of India produced this predictable result. Its the application to the village may well account for the following description of it by Monier-Williams:

It has existed almost unaltered since the description of its organization in Manu's code, two or three centuries before the Christian era. It has survived all the religious, political, and physical convulsions from which India has suffered from time immemorial. Invader after invader has ravaged the country with fire and sword; internal wars have carried devastation into every corner of the land; tyrannical oppressors have desolated its homesteads; famine has decimated its peasantry; pestilence has depopulated entire districts; floods and earthquakes have changed the face of nature; folly, superstition, and delusion have made havoc of all religion and morality—but the simple, self-contained Indian township has preserved its constitution intact, its customs, precedents, and peculiar institutions unchanged and unchangeable amid all other changes.[21]

One feature which came to be emphasized was the alleged absence of private property in pre-British India. This was based on a double error: for the preceding Muslim period of Indian history, this 'belief was based on a misunderstanding of the agrarian system of the Mughal empire by both Thomas Roe and François Bernier'.[22] while for the preceding Hindu period it was the 'emphasis on the village communities' which sustained this belief.[23] This culminated in the hands of Marxist thought in the formulation of the concept of the Asiatic Mode of Production:

The characteristics of the Asiatic Mode of Production were: the absence of privately owned land, since all land was state-owned; the predominantly village economy, the occasional town functioning more as a military camp than as a commercial centre, the nearly self-sufficient nature of this village economy with each isolated village meeting its agricultural needs and manufacturing essential goods; the lack of much surplus for exchange after the collection of a large percentage of the surplus by the State; the complete subjugation of the village communities to the State, made possible by state control of major public works, most importantly irrigation. The extraction of a maximum percentage of the surplus from the village communities enabled the despotic ruler to live in considerable luxury.[24]

The reification of caste as a category in Hindu sociology and its essentialist interpretation also seems to owe much to the proposition that Hindus lacked a sense of history. For history records change. From this it is but a step to the position—no history, no change. James Mill wrote: 'From the scattered hints, contained in the writings of the Greeks, the conclusion has been drawn that the Hindus, at the time of Alexander's invasion, were in a state of manners, society, and knowledge, exactly the same that in which they were discovered by the nations of modern Europe.'[25]

There is some truth in the charge: if it is 'a truism to say that legislation of today meets the social needs of yesterday' then it can be argued that 'the Hindu community continued to be governed by institutions moulded by laws which were codified 2,000 years ago and which were out of date even when they were codified'[26] on account of the truism just stated. 'The reason for this lack of direction of social ideals and the failure to prevent the growth of anti-social customs was undoubtedly the loss of political power.'[27] Thus the charge of a relatively static society holds to a degree but the reasons for it are no longer just cultural and have become historical in nature. Moreover, even the static character can be exaggerated.

When the great codes of Hindu Law were evolved, no doubt they represented the social forces of the time, but soon they had become antiquated. The succession of authoritative commentaries would show that the urge for modification was widely felt, and in the absence of a legislative authority, the method of a progressive interpretation by commentators in each succeeding generation was the only one available to Hindu thinkers.

The immutability of Hindu law and customs was never a principle with the authors of the great codes or their commentators. In fact the monumental volumes of Dr. Kane's *History of Dharma Sastra* would demonstrate clearly that in every age social thinkers tried to adjust Hindu institutions to the requirements of the time. If the laws are changeable it follows that the institutions, which are based on such laws, are equally changeable. The great weakness of Hindu society was not that the laws had remained immutable, but that the changes introduced have been spasmodic, local and dependent to a large extent on the ingenuity of individual commentators. They were not in any sense a continuous renovation of legal principles, not a legislative approximation to changing conditions.[28]

The importance of the proposition that the Hindus lacked a sense of history for understanding the economic realities of India becomes obvious as soon as one realizes that:

James Mill, who wrote the first great *History of British India*, was convinced that the Hindus had no history before the Muslims and they were always in the same abject, condition as that in which the British found them in Bengal in the eighteenth century.[29]

Religious Psychology

Some scholars have connected the proposition that the Hindus lacked a sense of history with Hindu religious psychology. Amaury de Riencourt is one of them. According to him:

If the history of the Indians is as shadowy as has already been pointed out on more than one occasion, it is largely because, of all the people on this earth, they were the least interested in history. The picture of India's historical development is as blurred as the development of the Indian soul is clear and sharply outlined. The key to an understanding of Indian Culture lies precisely in this total indifference toward history, toward the very process of time. Aryan India had no memory because she focused her attention on *eternity* not on time. Thus, the Indian world outlook developed in a direction diametrically opposed to China's for instance.[30]

According to him the 'most remarkable trait of Indian psychology is a complete, instinctive indifference to history and the preservation of historical records'.[31] Amaury de Riencourt's treatment of an incident in the life of Vivekananda is instructive on this point, wherein a psychological explanation is offered which pre-empts a potentially historical line of investigation. He writes:

It may be of interest to take note of a strange dream that haunted Vivekananda on his way back to India, a dream that could be analysed and perhaps interpreted as an unconscious reaction of the ahistorical Indian soul to the impact of history-conscious European Culture: an old man appeared to him and said: 'Observe carefully this place. It is the land where Christianity began. I am one of the therapeutic Essenes, who lived there. The truths and the ideas preached by us were presented as the teaching of Jesus. But Jesus the person was never born. Various proofs attesting this fact will be brought to light when this place is dug up.' Having awakened and informed himself of the location of the ship, Vivekananda was informed that they were fifty miles off the isle of Crete. Was it a prophetic dream or just the unconscious wish of a true Hindu soul? In any case, as his biographer added, 'for a spirit of his religious intensity ... the historic reality of God was the least of His realities.'[32]

PHILOSOPHY

The views of Hegel regarding to the academic status of Hindu philosophy have been very influential. Even those who have admitted that they are one-sided have not denied its influence.[33] It will be instructive to examine the role the proposition of the absence of a sense of history on part of the Hindus plays in his scheme. In order to do so, it is helpful to recognise some key aspects of Hegel's thought.

In Hegel's thought, system and history are combined, even integrated, in an unprecedented manner. The history of philosophy is the unfolding of philosophy itself, and Hegel's own system is designed as the consummation of the historical development of philosophy. System and history are the two sides of the self-manifestation of the spirit. We are what we have become in and through history.[34]

Moreover,

Hegel's scheme of the history of philosophy is primarily designed to deal with the history of European thought from Thales to Kant and Hegel himself. However, this is *not just one line of development among others*, Hegel's conception of 'Weltgeist' ('world spirit'), and the corresponding unity of the world-historical process, leaves no room for the assumption of other, independent or parallel streams of historical development. Where in this scheme does Asia, and India in particular, have its place?[35]

In Hegel's view 'Indian philosophy is inseparable from religion and the fundamental role of "substantiality" applies to philosophy as well as religion.'[36] The concept of substantiality is crucial here. By this Hegel refers to unity and ultimacy of one underlying 'substance' constituting the fundamental ontological premise. He identifies the Hindu *Brahman* as such, and Hindu thought accordingly for him is 'substantialist'. The description of Hindu thought as substantialist entails the following critique of it:

The Indian mind has thus found its way to the One and the Universal, which Hegel, too, sees as the true ground of religion and philosophy. But it has not found its way back to the concrete particularity of the world. It has not brought about a mediation and reconciliation of the universal and the particular, the one and the many. The finite is lost in the infinite; the world is lost in *Brahman*, which is the 'naught of all that is finite' ('das Nichts alles Endlichen'). The undivided unity of *brahman* and the multiplicity of the world do not and cannot affect or permeate each other. Regardless of all abstract assertions to the contrary, they are related to one another in unreconciled negation and exclusion: '... the One, just because it is entirely contentless and abstract, because it has not its particularizations in itself, lets them fall outside it, lets them escape in uncontrolled confusion.' This leads to the other extreme of Indian thought—its 'wild excesses of fantasy' ('wilde Ausschweifung der Phantasie'), an 'unrestrained frenzy' ('haltungsloser Taumel') of particulars, a rampant chaos of mythological and iconographic details. The Indian religion is not only 'religion of substance, it is also 'religion of fantasy' ('Religion der Phantasie').

According to Hegel, such constant oscillation between the 'supersensuous' and 'wildest sensuality' finds it most visible and striking expression in Indian art, and he refers to it repeatedly in his *Lectures on Aesthetics*. In his work, he also proposes his curious yet challenging thesis that the Indian way of thinking leaves no room for 'symbols' in the true and full sense of the word.[37]

... There is, in short, a lack of dialectical mediation: The absolute and infinite is not put to work in and for the finite and relative; and the relative and finite does not affect the infinite. Accordingly, there is no historical progress towards the enhancement of man and the world.

What appears as the ultimate depth of Indian thought is at the same time its essential defect: The finite and particular has not been transcended; rather, it has not been discovered and posited as such. According to Hegel, this discovery has been accomplished only by the 'hard European intellect'.[38]

The above presentation is that of Wilhelm Halbfass. Halbfass at least sometimes seems to imply that Hegel offered two views of Hindu thought, as when he writes:

Hegel's influence in the history and historiography of philosophy has been far-reaching and complex. However, his reception has often been one-sided and selective. Among historians of philosophy in the nineteenth century, Hegel's negative statements on India and the Orient in general, and his pronouncement that 'real philosophy' begins only in Greece, found wide acceptance, and they were taken as justification to dismiss Indian thought entirely from the historiography of philosophy, or to relegate it to a preliminary stage. The later statements that there is philosophy in the true and proper sense in India had virtually no impact; they were hardly ever noticed.[39]

Another factor must be mentioned. Whatever respect he had for the antiquity of Indian thought was also undermined when he discovered that the Hindus lacked a sense of history.

If we had formerly the satisfaction of believing in the antiquity of the Indian wisdom and holding it in respect, we now have ascertained through being acquainted with the great astronomical works of the Indians, the inaccuracy of all figures quoted. Nothing can be more confused, nothing more imperfect than the chronology of the Indians; no people which attained to culture in astronomy, mathematics, & c., is as incapable for history; in it they have neither stability nor coherence. It was believed that such was to be had at the time of Wikramaditya, who was supposed to have lived about 50 BC, and under whose reign the poet Kalidasa, author of Sakontala, lived. But further research discovered half a dozen Wikramadityas and careful investigation has placed his epoch in our eleventh century. The Indians have lines of kings and an enormous quantity of names, but everything is vague.[40]

The lasting significance of Hegel's interpretation may be judged from its influence on two thinkers: Christian Lassen and Karl Marx. Romila Thapar observes:

Hegel's philosophy of history influenced yet another interpretation of Indian history. Christian Lassen, writing in the mid-nineteenth century, applied the dialectic of thesis, antithesis, and synthesis—applied by Hegel to the phases of Greek, Roman, and Christian civilization in Europe—to India, where the three phases became Hindu, Muslim, and Christian civilization. Lassen tried in this way to connect Indian history with the general stream of world history in the common synthesis of Christian civilization. In addition, this idea further strengthened Mill's original periodization.[41]

She goes on to point out that 'in spite of applying the Hegelian dialectic to his interpretation of Indian history, Lassen was unable to refute Hegel's assumption regarding the unchanging nature of India's past.'[42] This same assumption was then 'taken up by Marx and worked into the thesis of the Asiatic Mode of Production' described earlier.[43]

Religion

The implications of the proposition that the Hindus were wanting in a sense of history for the depiction of the Hindu religious tradition are profound, for such a denial of history has the effect of shifting the focus on mythology and gives rise to the identification of the religion with its mythology.

It also had the effect of primitivizing the tradition, for the timeless mythic mode of perceiving the world was associated in the nineteenth century with what has been called a primitive mentality.

It also affected the way the tradition is understood at a more basic level. Malcolm Pitt writes:

Chronology is of comparatively little importance to the Hindu. It is no accident that the major great documents of Hinduism are not strictly speaking historical documents, as other great classics are. Even in the mythical stories in the biographies of the devotional saints of Hinduism, legend and fact are so intermingled that it is an almost impossible task for the historian today, either Indian or Western, to disentangle event from fiction.

It is this writer's conviction that a true understanding of the essence of Hinduism is not primarily the historian's job. It is interesting to note that in small essays about the size of this pamphlet Westerners would be very likely to take up the chronological development of Hinduism through its major documents and documentary periods, whereas the Indian would think of his total history as all one piece in relation to its major outlooks on life. The historian of religion can see the beginning, the development, and the flowering of certain aspects of Hinduism chronologically expressed. But as a religion not fundamentally grounded in history, and with the view of history as relatively unimportant, this development is interesting rather than essential.[44]

Art

The implication of such a view for the study of Hindu Art cannot be overlooked. As Heinrich von Stietencron notes:

It is one of the puzzling aspects of Indian sculpture in the pre-Muslim period that it seems to lack the glorification of earthly power, which is so prominent in many other cultures. In Hindu India, sculptural art is largely religious art. Representations abound of gods and their mythical actions, of saints, and seers, of sacred animals and holy plants. Secular scenes do exist, but they, too, form part of the decoration of temple walls or doorways. They are embedded into sacred space as part of the manifestations of the divine in a world—represented on the outer walls of the temple—which is permeated by, and dependent on, the power and eternal consciousness of the deity enshrined within.

The human sphere with its activities is depicted on the temple in many ways. Battles and hunting scenes, rituals and religious discourse, various domestic scenes, building activities, royal occupations and many other details of life occur. Symbols of fertility are abundantly present, and much has been written on the erotic element, which is so prominent on some of the temples.

Yet kings and queens—apart from a few exceptions—do not figure prominently on the temple walls, nor are major political events such as victories, treaties, etc., reproduced in stone imagery as a visible record of fame. Although the patrons of the artists were often kings or ministers or successful generals it is generally not their battles, which are represented; the battles shown are those of the heroes in the ancient epics of India. Moreover, images of kings, queens and donors, if available, are usually stylized to the degree of extinguishing individuality. To the modern viewer, therefore, there appears to be an a-historic and non-political attitude in indigenous Indian art, which, true to the alleged spiritual quest for the ultimate unchanging reality, did not bother to preserve in stone the transitory achievements of mortal kings.[45]

Heinrich von Stietencron no doubt proceeds to question this view, as demonstrated later on in the book. He, however, articulates the prevailing view in the history of Indian art, which is rooted in the proposition that the Hindus did not possess a sense of history.

Literature

The attribution of a historical view to the Hindus also has a bearing on our understanding of Hindu literature. The controversy between those who share the enthusiasm for the critical edition of the Mahābhārata, or those who do not, is illustrative in this respect.

This critical edition of the Mahābhārata was prepared at the Bhandarkar Oriental Research Institute at Poona by a group of scholars led by Vishnu S. Sukthankar over a period stretching from 1933–72. A. L. Basham seems to cite its preparation as an illustration of the fact that 'now the chief initiative in Indology comes from the Indians themselves'.[46] The point to note, however, is that although the initiative was Indian, its spirit was Western, inasmuch as the concept of determining a 'critical text' of a work is a Western notion. The Indic notion of an epic text, for instance, is of something which grows over time,[47] while the critical edition tried to determine the state of the text of the Mahābhārata as it might have been towards the end of the Gupta Period or c. 400 AD. Even some Western scholars like Madeleine Biardeau have opposed 'its very existence, arguing that all historical study of the Mahābhārata text as part of a search for coherent meaning is excluded automatically by the recognition of the epic's orally composed fluidity'.[48]

The contrasting attitudes of C. P. Brown and Kamal Zvelbil in this respect are also instructive. C. P. Brown comments on a lack of a sense of history on the part of Hindus as it relates to some forms of literary activity.

C. P. Brown, in constructing a Telugu dictionary, after several false starts decided to establish his corpus of lexical items by standardizing several texts, one of which was Manu Charitra. He assembled a group of learned assistants and collected upwards of a dozen manuscript versions of the texts. These manuscripts, he wrote, 'swarmed with errors', which his assistants 'adjusted by guess as they went along'. Brown had copies made of each manuscript, leaving alternative pages blank with the verses numbered. He had a number of clerks with several copies of the manuscript in front of them, as well as 'three professors', masters of 'grammar and prosody, both Sanskrit and Telagu'. The verses were then read out, discussed by the pundits, with Brown deciding which version was correct, 'just as a judge frames a decree out of conflicting evidence'.

Brown, through this procedure, was creating what he thought of as an 'authentic' text. With the advent of printing in India, which was simultaneously developing along with the European ideas about how texts were constituted and transmitted, this was to have a powerful effect in standardizing the Telugu language and its literature. Implicit in this process were several European assumptions about literature. In European theory texts have authors who create or record what had previously been transmitted orally or through writing. Before the advent of printing it was assumed that texts 'swarmed with errors' because of the unreliability of the scribes, leading to the corruption of the original and pure version created by the author.[46]

By contrast, Kamal Zvelbil takes a more charitable view. As Bernard Cohn notes:

Europeans in the nineteenth century saw literature as being conditioned by history, with an author building on and knowing great works of thought which he or she, through an act of genius and originality, could affect. Kamal Zvelbil has recently argued that Indians do not order their literature in a temporal linear fashion, but rather by structures and type. Literature in India 'has a simultaneous existence and composes a simultaneous order'. He has also pointed out that persons are constituted differently in India than in the West. In India they are less unique individuals and more incumbents of positions in a social order which has pre-existed them and which will continue to exist after their deaths. A poet or writer before the nineteenth century, Zvelbil states, did not invent or create a poem or a literary work, rather they could only express 'an unchanging truth in a traditional form' and by following 'traditional rules'.[47]

In sum, then, hardly any aspect of Indological studies has been left untouched by the assumption that the Hindus lacked a sense of history.

End Notes

1. Governor-General Marques of Hastings (1813–23) observed: 'The Hindoo appears a being nearly limited to mere animal functions ... with no higher intellect

than a dog and an elephant, or a monkey ... such a people can at no period have been more advanced in civil polity' (cited by R. C. Majumdar, 'India's Influence on the Thought and Culture of the World Through the Ages', in R. C. Majumdar, ed., *Swami Vivekananda Centenary Memorial Volume* [Calcutta: Swami Vivekananda Centenary, 1965], p. 1).

2. Cited by Sheldon Pollock, 'Rāmāyaṇa and the Political Imagination in India', *The Journal of Asian Studies* 52:2:292 (May 1993).

3. Cited in Troy Wilson Organ, *The Hindu Quest For the Perfection of Man* (Athens, Ohio: Ohio University, 1970), p. 30, note 68.

4. Ibid.

5. Benjamin Walker, *The Hindu World* (New York & Washington: Frederick A. Praeger, 1968), Vol. I, p. 455.

6. Troy Wilson Organ, op. cit., p. 31.

7. R. C. Majumdar, 'Indian History, Its Nature, Scope and Method', in R. C. Majumdar, ed., *The Vedic Age* (London: George Allen & Unwin, 1952), p. 41.

8. Ibid., p. 38.

9. Troy Wilson Organ, op. cit., p. 31.

10. Amaury de Reincourt, *The Soul of Indiâ* (New Delhi: Sterling Publishers Private Ltd., 1986) pp. 9–10.

11. K. Satchidananda Murty, *Vedic Hermeneutics* (Delhi: Motilal Banarsidass, 1993), p. 26.

12. 'Alberuni's India', although a great work, is not flawless. It describes the Pāṇḍavas as being four rather than five in number (Edward C. Sachau, ed., *Alberuni's India* [London: Kegan Paul, Trench, Trubner and Co., 1914] Vol. I, p. 108); confuses the word *mātrāḥ* with *mātaraḥ* in another context (ibid., Vol. I, p. 42); and states that the *Aśvamedha* involved the sacrifice of a mare (ibid., Vol. II, p. 139) which would make a mockery of a well-known if obscene ritual which constitutes part of it (see Stephanie W. Jamison, *Sacrificed Wife / Sacrificer's Wife* [New York and Oxford: Oxford University Press, 1996], pp. 65–72).

13. Wilhelm Halbfass, *India and Europe: An Essay in Understanding* (Albany, NY: SUNY Press, 1988), pp. 25–6.

14. H. G. Rawlinson, *India: A Short Cultural History* (revised) (London: The Cresset Press, 1954 [1937]), p. 3. Rawlinson is however not entirely correct about the memory of Aśoka being lost altogether. Shankar Goyal points out that the Ādiparva of the Mahābhārata 'mentions King Aśoka who is said to have been an incarnation of Mahāsura and is described as of great power and invincible' (op. cit., p. 4).

15. Ibid., p. 393.

16. K. M. Panikkar, *The Foundations of New India* (London: George Allen & Unwin Ltd., 1963), p. 67.

17. Wilhelm Halbfass, op. cit., p. 93.

18. Cited in Ronald Inden, *Imagining India* (Bloomington and Indianapolis: Indiana University Press, 2000 [1990]), p. 20.

19. S. Krishnaswami Aiyangar, *Ancient India and South Indian History and Culture* (Poona: Oriental Book Agency, 1941), Vol. 1, p. 31.

20. Romila Thapar, *Ancient Indian Social History: Some Interpretations* (New Delhi: Orient Longman, 1978), p. 6. Romila Thapar goes on to say (ibid.): 'This concept was not new to European thinking on Asia. Its roots can perhaps be traced to the writings of Herodotus, to the Greco-Persian antagonism in the ancient world, and to the pronouncements of Aristotle on the nature of kingship and political systems in Asia. It was taken up and developed into a political theory by Montesquieu in *L'Esprit des lois*, and this theory was debated by the French Physiocrats and by Voltaire, who found it unacceptable. But the concept became established in the nineteenth century when it was introduced into various philosophies of history and was thus given intellectual legitimacy.'

21. Cited in Ronald Inden, op. cit., p. 134.

22. Romila Thapar, op. cit., p. 6.

23. Ibid., p. 7.

24. Ibid.

25. James Mill, op. cit., p. 35.

26. K. M. Panikkar, *The Foundations of New India*, p. 33.

27. Ibid., p. 34.

28. Ibid., pp. 33–4.

29. Ibid., p. 67.

30. Amaury de Reincourt, op. cit., p. 15.

31. Ibid., p. 9.

32. Ibid., pp. 236–7.

33. Wilhelm Halbfass, op. cit., p. 417.

34. Ibid., p. 87.

35. Ibid., p. 88, emphasis added.

36. Ibid., p. 89.

37. Ibid., pp. 89–90.

38. Ibid., p. 90.

39. Ibid., pp. 98–9.

40. G. W. F. Hegel, *Lectures in Philosophy of History*, tr. E. S. Haldane (Nebraska: University of Nebraska Press, 1995), Vol. I, pp. 125–6.

41. Romila Thapar, op. cit., pp. 6–7.

42. Ibid., p. 7.

43. Ibid.

44. Malcolm Pitt, *Introducing Hinduism* (New York: Friendship Press, 1955), p. 20.

45. Heinrich von Stietencron, 'Political Aspects of Indian Religious Art', *Visible Religion,* Vols IV, V (Brill: Leiden, 1985/86), p. 16.

46. A. L. Basham, op. cit., p. 8.

47. M. A. Mehendale, 'Language and Literature', in R. C. Majumdar, ed., *The Age of Imperial Unity* (fourth edition) (Bombay: Bharatiya Vidya Bhavan, 1968), p. 246.

48. Ruth Cecily Katz, *Arjuna in the Mahābhārata: Where Krishna Is, There is Victory* (Delhi: Motilal Banarsidass, 1990), p. 25, note 58.

49. Bernard S. Cohn, 'The Command of Language And the Language of Command', in Ranjit Guha, ed., *Writings on South Asian History and Society* (Delhi: Oxford University Press, 1985), pp. 324–5.

50. Ibid., p. 325.

Hindu Responses to the View that Hindus Have No Sense of History

I

Those Hindus who have not chosen to dismiss the assessment that they lack a sense of history with a Nietzschean shrug of the shoulder that 'only the dead have a history', have responded variously to the proposition that the Hindus lacked a sense of history. The Hindu response to this proposition has been mild, despite its serious consequences. Apart from being mild, it has also been varied.

(1) One line of response was simply an admission of the fact, accompanied by praise for Western scholarship, for having restored the history of Hinduism to the Hindus. A good representative of this school is K. M. Panikkar. He writes:

The creation of a Hindu historiography and the recovery of India's great past constitute the most spectacular, as also the first fundamental contribution of European scholarship to India. In the century that passed between the acceptance of the identification of Sandrocottus of Alexander's history with Chandra Gupta Maurya and the discovery of the Indus valley civilization lies the great romance of the rediscovery of India's past and the creation of a national self-image for the Hindus as one of the creative civilizing peoples of the world with a continuous history of 3,000 years. The works of scholars like Princep Bothilingk [*sic*], of excavators and archaeologists like Alexander Cunningham and Marshall, of students of literature, religion and culture like Sir William Jones, Max Muller [*sic*] and A. B. Keith opened up to the astonished eyes of Indians themselves a continuous history of political, social and cultural activity which was not inferior to that of other contemporary civilizations. Also, European scholars working in Central Asia, China and SouthEast Asia recovered the astonishing history of ancient Indian cultural expansion, which established

Hinduized kingdoms and empires in the Pamirs, in Malaya, in the Indonesian archipelago, and the fertile valleys of the Mekong.[1]

He goes on to say:

All this reconstruction of India's past and the translation and popularization of great Indian philosophical and religious classics was the work almost exclusively of European scholars: English, German, French, Swedish, Russian, in fact scholars from every part of Europe. It was only in the last decades of the nineteenth century that Indian scholarship began to participate effectively in this work. The foundation of the Asiatic Society of Bengal by Sir William Jones, poet, scholar and judge, the decipherment of the Asokan inscriptions, opening up the vista of ancient history from records preserved in stone, metals and coins, the discovery of Ankor Vat in the overgrown jungles of Cambodia, the exploration of Central Asian caves by Stein, Pelliot and others, and finally the excavations at Mohenjodaro—these are but the most sensational events of a truly thrilling story of the rediscovery of a lost intellectual world through the disinterested work of foreign scholars. Nor should one forget to mention the massive achievements of men in the different Universities of Europe and later of America—Oxford, Cambridge, Paris, Heidelberg, Leyden, Harvard—who through love of learning translated, interpreted and published the vast literature which lay buried in Sanskrit and Pali, thereby opening up not only to the West but to the new middle classes in India itself an immense and almost unknown realm of religious thought and artistic achievement.[2]

He then goes on to point out that this historical debt may possess a political component as well.

The question may legitimately be asked whether there would have been an Indian nationalism if this recovery of India's past and the consequent creation of an Indian national image had not been achieved through the work of European scholars. The answer to this question is clear. There would undoubtedly have developed national movements in India, but not on the basis of only two nations dominantly Hindu and Muslim but of many regional states, the Marathas, the Andhras, the Bengalis and others. Without a Hindu ideology, picturing the Hindu people as one, which Western scholarship and historiography enabled Hindus to create and develop, the alternative would have been the growth of regional nationalism based on recent and still remembered histories. India in fact would have been balkanized into numerous states each cherishing a nationalism of its own and not recognizing the common nationhood.[3]

K. M. Panikkar's response may contain elements of overstatement. The extent to which such reconstruction was 'almost exclusively the work of European scholars' may be questioned as they often worked with native assistants.[4] Similarly, one might question how disinterested the enterprise really was, from a post-colonial perspective.[5] One might also wish to recognize the pan-Indian nature of 'Hindu nationalism' independently of the British Period.[6] Nevertheless, Panikkar's view does represent one major type of response.

(2) A second type of response also seems to basically accept the proposition but with more reservations. R. C. Majumdar represents a good example of this response. He writes:

> The absence of any regular historical chronicle is the leading feature of this period. When we consider the vast mass of contemporary literature and its extremely wide range, the almost utter lack of historical texts certainly appears as a somewhat strange phenomenon. Some people are, therefore, inclined to believe that such literature did exist, and explain its absence by a theory of wholesale destruction. It must be regarded, however, as extremely singular that the agencies of destruction should have singled out this particular branch of literature as their special target. But the strongest argument against the supposed existence of regular historical literature is the absence of any reference to historical texts. We have, therefore, to admit that the literary genius of India, so fertile and active in almost all conceivable branches of study was not applied to chronicling the records of kings and the rise and fall of states and nations. It is difficult to give a rational explanation of this deficiency, but the fact admits of no doubt.

Majumdar then attempts an explanation of this deficiency, and finds that it defies full explanation.

> The deficiency is all the more strange as there are indications that the ancient Indians did not lack in historical sense. This is proved by the carefully preserved lists of teachers in various Vedic texts, as well as in writings of the Buddhists, Jains and other religious sects. That this spirit also extended to the political field is shown not only by the songs and poems in praise of kings and heroes referred to in Vedic literature, but also by the practice of reciting eulogies of kings and royal families on ceremonial occasions. Even so late as the seventh century AD Hiuen Tsang [=Xuanzang] that each province in India had its own official for maintaining written records in which were mentioned good and evil events, with calamities and fortunate occurrences. That this practice continued for centuries after Hiuen Tsang is proved by a large number of local chronicles and the preambles in old land grants, which record the genealogies of royal families, sometimes for several generations.

Further attempts to explain the deficiency in historiography are no more successful.

> We may thus presume that neither historical sense nor historical material was altogether wanting in ancient India. What was lacking was either the enthusiasm or the ability to weave the scattered raw materials into a critical historical text with a

proper literary setting, which the people would not willingly let die. In other words, in spite of great intellectual and literary activity, India did not produce a Herodotus or Thucydides, not even a Livy or Tacitus. It has been argued that this was partly due to the peculiar temperament of the people who, to use the words of Hiuen Tsang 'made light of the things of the present world'. But this explanation can be hardly regarded as satisfactory when we remember the great progress of the Indians in various branches of secular literature, including law, political science, and the art of administration.[7]

Majumdar then brings these considerations to bear on the discussion of a text, which comes closest to being a history in Sanskrit literature. This is the *Rājataraṅgiṇī* of Kalhaṇa.

It is a history of Kashmir, written throughout in verse, by Kalhaṇa in AD 1149–50. This is the only work in ancient Indian literature that may be regarded as an historical text in the true sense of the word. The author has not only taken great pains to collect his material from the existing chronicles and other sources but, at the beginning of his work, he has laid down a few general principles for writing history which are remarkable as being far in advance of his age. Indeed they may be regarded as anticipating, to a large extent, the critical method of historical research, which was not fully developed till the nineteenth century AD. In view of the lamentable paucity of historical talent in ancient India, it is worth while quoting a few of Kalhaṇa's observations, showing the high level which the Indian intellect had attained even in this much neglected sphere of activity. Regarding the strict impartiality to be observed by an historian Kalhaṇa remarks:

'That virtuous poet alone is worthy of praise who, free from love or hatred, ever restricts his language to the exposition of facts' (I.7).

As to the method of collecting data we may quote the following verses among others (I.14, 15):

'I have examined eleven works of former scholars which contain the chronicles of the kings, as well as the views of the sage Nīla (*Nīlapurāṇa*).'

'By the inspection of ordinances (*śāsana*) of former kings relating to religious foundations and grants, laudatory inscriptions (*praśasti-patra*) as well as written records (*śāstra*), all wearisome error has been set at rest.'[8]

(3) Yet another response has been to propose that this lack of historical sense was meant to achieve a historical goal—the unification of the Indian people. This would imply that the absence of a historical sense was deliberately cultivated to further social and political ends. This seems to be one implication of the following remarks of Madhav Deshpande. He writes:

What has this 'unhistorical history' done to India? The historians of modern times look at Manu and others with a contempt, which is similar to the contempt expressed against the rewriting of history done by the communist thinkers. A Russian version of Russian history appears to be too coloured to an American historian and he vows to write a matter-of-fact history of Russia. A nation's history has often been subjected to the 'designs' of the historian and his socio-political background. If Manu was not writing a critical history of the Indian peoples, did he have any 'designs' of his own which might have forced him to adjust the historical facts to fit his purpose? S. K. Chatterji talks about the 'Hindu Reconstruction of Ancient Hindu History'. He points out that 'a significant point in this reconstruction is that the great fact of different races of people having brought in diverse elements of Hindu culture... has not been taken note of either unwillingly, or deliberately and with a purpose.' We certainly do not know the real cause of Manu's failure to take note of the facts of Indian history, as our modern historians perceive it. However, the historical impact of this 'unhistoric history' has been quite significant.

He goes on to point out:

By failing to recognize the foreign and racially different origins of the different peoples in India, and by focusing on their synchronic socio-religious positions, rights and duties, the classical Indian tradition brought about a wonderful racial and cultural synthesis of Indian peoples. 'Ignorance is bliss', a modern historian may comment in despair. However, for one who aims at such a synthesis, willful ignoring, and not ignorance, may indeed serve a grand practical purpose. As Chatterji puts it: 'Here was a deliberate sacrifice of history for a larger issue. And this larger issue was the reconstruction of a new historical standpoint, in which peoples of various races and colours and languages were looked upon as limbs of a single body, a body which came to be felt as an organic whole.' The synchronic feeling of socio-religious unity was more important than the historical fact of diverse origins, and therefore, to serve a synchronic purpose, the synchronic unity had to be projected back into history to the first acts of creation.[9]

Madhav Despande then proceeds to contrast the effect of such a historicity with the results that flow from modern historical research.

In comparison with the historical impact on Indian society of the 'unhistorical histories' reconstructed by Manu and other classical writers, the impact of modern academic scholarship and history on Indian society is quite divisive. Modern historical scholarship has destroyed the grand designs of Manu. If historians have done a great service to their own fields, their conclusions have had an enormous socio-political impact in India. While classical India never saw the Aryan-Dravidian racial and cultural tensions, the Aryan-Dravidian linguistic identities and political conflicts became stronger after the publication of Robert Caldwell's *Comparative Grammar of Dravidian Languages* in the middle of the nineteenth century. The forgotten historic and prehistoric divisions were resurrected to divide a culturally unified subcontinent. The destruction of the ignorance of the historical diversity lead to the destruction of the unity based on that purposeful ignorance.[10]

One could thus argue that the Hindus preferred a deliberately cultivated lack of history over a sense for it, because they did not wish to make the past the enemy of the present. This point can be illustrated with the help of the Bhaviṣya Purāṇa (II:22.13,14). It contains a reference apparently to King Akbar of the Mughal Dynasty. According to this account a young Brahmin, seeing the entire earth overrun by *mlecchas* or foreign rulers, decided to burn himself upon a pyre in order to be reborn as a *kṣatriya* or warrior-king, in order to rid the earth of foreign rulers. However, on account of an error in the ritual undertaken to secure such a birth, he was himself reborn as a mleccha or impure foreigner, namely, Akbar. This is obviously a metempsychotic attempt on the part of some anonymous author at legitimizing the rapprochement between the Hindus and the Muslims initiated by Akbar.

Just as Madhav Despande had argued the Hindus might have turned the alleged lack of a sense of history to mythical-cum-sociological advantage, here we see it turned to mythic-cum-historical advantage. Some implications of such manoeuvres take on a new significance when such a classical view of history begins to privilege an 'imaginary past'.

> While the early western scholars of Vedic literature concluded that the Vedas were produced by 'primitive' peoples and that later the Indian religion developed into a 'non-primitive' form, the traditional Hindus cannot accept such conceptions. For them, the Vedic Aryans are the ultimate authority in every matter, and hence they must be at least as much 'developed' as the modern Hindus, if not more. The Hindu theory of declining ages combined with the notion of the authority of the past for the present leads to an inevitable construction of a more developed and a more glorious past. A primitive past cannot be considered to be an authority for the developed present. This is the western conception of history. In the Hindu conception, the past must have been more developed than the present, since the past is the authority for the present. This conceptual conflict played an important role in the history of modern India. The concept of 'progress' was declined by different groups in different ways. For some 'progress' meant getting away from the old Indian ideas and moving toward westernization. However, a significant number of Indian élites defined 'progress' as a movement towards achieving the heights of the glorious past. Thus a conception of welfare states expressed in the term Rāmarājya 'the kingdom of Rāma' is a modern attempt at recreating a golden age in the past.[11]

It is important to recognize such an implication of ahistoricizing history. Its importance will become clear while discussing another strand of Hindu response in due course.

(4) Yet another response took the same view—that the lack of a sense of

history serves a higher purpose in Hinduism but this time a moral one. Mahatma Gandhi seems to have taken such a view of the matter. We noted earlier the curious fact, and perhaps a further testimony to the truth of the proposition itself, that when the Hindus were charged, as it were, with lacking a sense of history and lacking in historiography, that they did not seem particularly perturbed by such a charge and almost seemed to accept it cheerfully. They even tried to turn the charge to advantage. In evidence of this one may cite the following passage from Mahatma Gandhi's *Hind Swaraj*, a book which he wrote at the age of forty, originally in Gujarati, in 30,000 words by hand, and ambidextrously when one hand began to fail, in the course of a voyage from England to South Africa between 13 and 22 November 1909. This is a book about which Gokhale thought Gandhi would himself consign to the flames as hastily conceived, but of which Gandhi himself wrote, years later, that 'except for withdrawing the word 'prostitute' used in connection with the British Parliament which annoyed an English lady, I wish to make no change at all.' The following passage therein, which occurs in the course of an imaginary dialogue between a person called the Reader and an Editor is relevant for our concerns:

READER: Is there any historical evidence as to the success of what you have called soul-force or truth-force? No instance seems to have happened of any nation having risen through soul-force. I still think that the evildoers will not cease doing evil without physical punishment.

EDITOR: The poet Tulsidas has said: 'Of religion, pity, or love, is the root, as egotism of the body. Therefore, we should not abandon pity so long as we are alive.' This appears to me to be a scientific truth. I believe in it as much as I believe in two and two being four. The force of love is the same as the force of the soul or truth. We have evidence of its working at every step. The universe would disappear without the existence of that force. But you ask for historical evidence. It is, therefore, necessary to know what history means. The Gujarati equivalent means: 'It so happened.' If that is the meaning of history, it is possible to give copious evidence. But if it means the doings of kings and emperors, there can be no evidence of soul-force or passive resistance in such history. You cannot expect silver ore in a tin mine. History, as we know it, is a record of the wars of the world, and so there is a proverb among Englishmen that a nation, which has no history, that is, no wars, is a happy nation. How kings played, how they became enemies of one another, how they murdered one another, is found accurately recorded in history, and if this were all that had happened in the world, it would have been ended long ago. If the story of the universe had commenced with wars, not a man would have been found alive today. Those people who have been warred against have disappeared as, for instance, the natives of Australia of which hardly a man was left alive by the intruders. Mark, please, that these natives did not use soul-force in self-defense, and it does not require much foresight to know that the Australians will share the same fate as their victims. 'Those that take the sword shall perish by the sword.' With us the proverb is that professional swimmers will find a watery-grave.

The fact that there are so many men still alive in the world shows that it is based not on the force of arms but on the force of truth or love. Therefore, the greatest and most unimpeachable evidence of the success of this force is to be found in the fact that, in spite of the wars of the world, it still lives on.

Thousands, indeed tens of thousands, depend for their existence on a very active working of this force. Little quarrels of millions of families in their daily lives disappear before the exercise of this force. Hundreds of nations live in peace. History does not and cannot take note of this fact. History is really a record of every interruption of the even working of the force of love or of the soul. Two brothers quarrel; one of them repents and re-awakens the love that was lying dormant in him; the two again begin to live in peace; nobody takes note of this. But if the two brothers, through the intervention of solicitors or some other reason take up arms or go to law which is another form of the exhibition of brute force,—their doings would be immediately noticed in the Press, they would be the talk of their neighbours and would probably go down to history. And that is true of families and communities is true of nations. There is no reason to believe that there is one law for families and another for nations. History, then, is a record of an interruption of the course of nature. Soul-force, being natural, is not noted in history.[12]

It is clear that the absence of history here has been turned to moral advantage. It has been proposed that Mahatma Gandhi may have started out with such a concept of history but that his attitude to it changed with the passage of time, and that by 1937 he was ready to make history rather than overlook it. B. Ganguli writes:

Whereas generally history is a chronicle of kings and their wars the future history is the history of man ... he was gripped by the present when he said: 'We are the makers of our destiny. We can mend and mar the present and on that depends the future. Our past holds us, he said, but like all other doctrines this may well be ridden to death.'[13]

Mahatma Gandhi also obviously believed in historical transformation. He said: 'History provides us with a whole series of miracles of masses of people being converted to a particular viewpoint in the twinkling of an eye.'[14]

In his case perhaps the miracle he hoped for was the conversion to non-violence. It is thus possible to argue in terms of the Heideggarian thesis of the 'Europeanization of the earth' that Gandhi's concept of history was also getting Europeanized.[15] However, even here Gandhi was perhaps looking for 'the permanent, the truth in history, the philosophical structure and the meaning, the purpose of history, as distinguished from the ceaseless flux of the historical process'.[16]

(5) Another view associates this lack of a sense of history with the *empirical* orientation of the Hindu tradition, and turns it to religious and philosophical advantage by grabbing the bull by the horns, as it were, a feat Professor D. S. Sarma seems to perform in the opening paragraph of his book entitled *Hinduism Through the Ages*. He writes:

> One of the characteristics of ancient Hindu thought is its indifference to history. In discussing the contents of a book, for instance, ancient and even mediaeval Indian writers care very little for the date or the life of the author. They care more for the truth of experience or the soundness of doctrine than the circumstances that gave it birth. What Sir Charles Eliot says of the religious mind in general is particularly applicable to them. 'The truly religious mind does not care for the history of religion, just as, among us, the scientific mind does not dwell on the history of science.' But there is no doubt that the Hindu writers went to one extreme in ignoring history altogether while modern western writers go to the other extreme in making too much of the historical treatment of thought and art and digging at the roots of a tree instead of enjoying its flower and fruit. What we term history may, no doubt, be far from the many-sided reality which it seeks to record. It may too often be only a very faulty and subjective view of events. All the same, the historical treatment of a subject, however imperfect and one-sided it may be, has its own value. The historical treatment of a religion has its value even for the most religious of men.[17]

This position also finds a mild echo in the view that 'to them [that is, Indians] the facts themselves were always more important than their chronological order, and that they attached no importance at all, specially in literary matters, to the question of what was earlier or later.'[18]

Another version of this response also recognizes the isomorphism of this approach to history with that of the scientist. Ashis Nandy refers to that Indian 'attitude to history' which

> Reduces men and events to data and statistics, so as to neutralize any emotion that may be associated with them. The aim is to dissociate affect from cognition and indirectly express the former through a manifestly desiccated recital of figures and events. That it why, in traditional Indian historiography, the data produced and the statistic used are often so unique. A king is mentioned as having sixty thousand children, and the heavens are mentioned as being inhabited by three hundred and thirty million gods, not only to make the point that the king is potent and the gods are many, but also to wipe out what many would consider the real data, and obviate any possibility of verification or empirical treatment. If you have sixty thousand children,

no one cares to ask their names or whereabouts, not even the one-minded orientalist; and no sacred text need list the three hundred million gods, even for the priest. In fact, it is expected that you do not take these figures seriously. You can only counterpoise against these communications others more potent. In other words, in this type of historiography, data are important only so far as they relate to the overall logic and the cultural symbols that must be communicated.[19]

The reader will note the opposite senses in which the word 'empirical' can be employed in discussing this point. When it is claimed that Hindu tradition is empirical, what is meant is that it is results-oriented and that according to many schools and sects of Hinduism the state of spiritual felicity can be experienced in this very life.[20] In such a context a seeker or a Guru becomes a 'type' and the type of experience one has, or aims for, is transcendental and meta-*empirical*, that is, not of this empirical world, the sense in which science uses the term. It is with this in the background that one might wish to savour the convergence between Hinduism and science on this point as noticed by Ashis Nandy.

> The more historical detail, whether of science's present or its past, or more responsibility to the historical details that are presented could only give artificial status to human idiosyncrasy, error and confusion .... The depreciation of historical fact is deeply and probably functionally ingrained in the ideology of the scientific profession, the same profession that places the highest of all values upon factual details of other sorts.[21]

(6) Another approach views this deficiency from the perspective of Yoga, or turns it to spiritual advantage, as it were. Professor T. S. Rukmani observed in the course of her inaugural address, when she assumed the Chair in Hinduism at the University of Durban-Westville, on 18 August 1994:

> However, it would be in the fitness of things, to point out two important pathways among many others, which the ancient Hindu seers felt would help one in the realization of one's growth towards unity consciousness. The first of these is a total submergence of the individual in the totality of existence, even to the extent of anonymity. This is the reason for the oft-quoted statement that the ancient Indian had no sense of history, meaning thereby, that there was no indication of the date of the lives of individual authors, artists, painters, sculptors and others. Combined with this was the second principle of cultivating an attitude of detachment, even in the midst of attachment. A little reflection will make clear the close connection between these two principles. Thus one of the Upanisads proclaims—*īśāvāsyamidaṁ sarvaṁ yatkiṁca jagatyām jagat, tena tyaktena bhuñjithā mā gṛdhaḥ kasyasvit dhanam*—i.e., while the world exists as common to all individuals as God-given or given by nature, as individuals we have the responsibility to enjoy 'by renouncing' and not by

indulging or over indulging ourselves. This attitude of renunciation can only be realized when there is the understanding of how little, in an absolute sense, a human being really is, and how 'if the self is not widened into the universal spirit,' as Radhakrishnan says, 'the values themselves become subjective and the self itself will collapse into nothing.' This brings us back to what we began with, i.e., the dialectic of the centre and the circumference, which is the only way to come to an understanding of life in its many divergent forms and in its essence.[22]

This could well be one implication of the fact that philosophy and religion have not diverged in India the way they have in the West.[23]

(7) Yet others have tried to turn the alleged lack of a sense of history among the Hindus to mythic advantage. The Hindu dwells in a cosmic and mythic world, where in an undisclosed but vaguely Eliadean manner the terror of time and history is overcome. Echoes of such a view can be heard in a passage such as the following from the pen of one of India's leading cultural historians, Professor G. C. Pande:

> The whole world-view of the ancient Vedic age consistently superimposes the mythical on the historical because it seeks to understand the realities of human life in terms of celestial paradigms.[24]

Those who subscribed to the school of perennial philosophy were bemused by the West's fascination with history, from which they felt India was gratefully free. The more apocalyptic among them saw in the West's fascination with history even a sign that it is about to go under, on the analogy of the person about to drown who sees his or her whole life flash past before disappearing in the waters. With this in mind, some scholars distinguish between secular and 'sacred' history. Perhaps anxious not to give offence to the Hindus by denying them any sense of history they identify the presence of 'sacred history' among them. Just as when the geography of a text, upon failing to conform to actual geography, may be described as 'sacred geography', statements claiming to be historical but not being so could courteously and euphemistically be described as 'sacred history'. There is some of this in the use of the term 'sacred history', but there is also more to it. Ainslie T. Embree writes, for instance:

> The Hindu tradition, which is so rich in many varieties of literature, has remarkably little historical literature of the kind found in comparable periods either in Europe or China, but it does possess a vast amount of writing that deals in a special way with the past. This is the literature known as the Purāṇas, a class of texts that is included in the canon of scripture, although of a lesser degree of sanctity and authority than the Vedic writings. They are not histories in the modern usage of the term, nor are they

even comparable to medieval chronicles, but they are sacred history, providing accounts of the origin of the universe, the deeds of the gods, and the genealogies of ancient kings.[25]

But this concept of 'sacred history' does possess its own profile. Ainslie T. Embree explains:

While it is impossible to speak of a 'Hindu view of history', since this phrase implies a way of looking at the world that was foreign to Indian thought, there is, however, an understanding of the nature of the historical process that is of fundamental importance for the Hindu tradition. The principal feature of this understanding, which is given an elaborate analysis in the Purāṇas, is that human existence must be seen against a background of an almost unimaginable duration of time. In contrast to other civilizations which have been content to see man's history in terms of thousands of years, Indians—Buddhists and Jains as well as Hindus—spoke of billions of years. But even these figures, which are nearly meaningless in their magnitude, are dwarfed by the concept of cycles of aeons, endlessly renewing themselves, without beginning or end. Time and the historical process are parts of a vast cyclical movement, but not, as in some cyclical versions of history, a simple cycle of birth, growth, death and then rebirth with a repetition of the past. The Hindu model is of concentric circles, moving within each other in a complex series of retrogressive movements. The vastest cycle was 'a year of Brahmā' which by some reckonings was 311,040,000 million years long, with Brahmā's life lasting for one hundred of these cycles. This was followed by dissolution of all the worlds—those of men and gods—and then creation once more took place.

The matter does not end here.

Within these cycles there were other cycles, which were of more imaginable dimensions, and it is these, which are of primary significance for human history. A *kalpa*, or day of Brahmā, was 4,320 million years long, and within this were the smallest cycles, the four *yugas*. The *Krita Yuga*, the golden age, lasted for 1,728,000 years; the *Tretā,* for 1,296,000 years; the *Dvāpara* for 864,000 years; and the *Kali* for 432,000 years. The four ages are calculated as a descending arithmetical progression, marked by progressive physical and spiritual deterioration. Present history is taking place within the *Kali Yuga*, which explains the violence and evil of human history. When this age comes to an end, a new cycle will begin—one of the thousand cycles of yugas that make up a day of Brahmā.

Man cannot save the social process from the decay and dissolution that is an inherent part of its structure, but he can save himself from within the process. The point is made, indeed, that one mark of the wickedness of the *Kali Yuga* is that salvation has been made much easier than in the former ages, since men of this age could not be expected to fulfill the rigorous requirements of a better time.[26]

(8) Some may be said to react to the proposition that Hinduism lacks a

sense of history not by deploring this fact but encouraging its acceptance for the sake of arriving at a proper understanding of Hinduism. David Shulman writes:

The problems posed by our materials are well known; we can continue to cling to the path of Herodotus, categorically sifting fact from fable, myth, or legend, but with rather unsatisfactory results. At some point our understanding of Hinduism should incorporate an Indian epistemology as well as sensitivity to the inner world of the actors, viewed, of course, with our analytic concerns. Are there shared symbolic means of expressing this inner world? What are the limits?[27]

He goes on to say:

E.V. Daniel has recently argued that South Indian culture has a predilection for the iconic (in Peirce's usage). What implications does this have for the definition of the self and of the other? For processes of institution building, for the state, for religious variety and change? If India blurs the boundary between 'history' and 'myth' (all *itihāsa*)—the distinction so beloved of Western historiography—do we not distort by drawing in sharp contours? Romila Thapar has been working on such questions (the semantics of *itihāsa*), which draw upon the old Weberian framework of analysis. Perhaps Hinduism can mean a certain definable set of cultural processes, a dynamic of possible transformations (rather than a set of stable features)—as an Indian view might naturally suggest. I have argued that the dialectic of *pravṛtti-nivṛtti* may help us to understand certain aspects of the medieval South Indian state; this is one example of the tradition's potential contribution to our external interpretative constructions. One might also imagine an *ālaṅkārika* vision of Hinduism and its history, with stress on *lakṣaṇā* or *vakrokti*, or processes of suggestion. All this without sacrificing our objectivity, or our concern with 'factuality'. Reconsidering Hinduism means reconsidering our usual categories and meanings. We have to address the challenge implicit in Obeyesekere's remark in his work on Pattini: 'A historiography that relies exclusively on well-documented and incontrovertible historical evidence, such as evidence from inscriptions, must surely be wrong, since it assumes that the *recorded* data must be the *significant* data shaping history and controlling the formation and transformation of the institutions of a people.'[28]

(9) Some have drawn attention to the special nature of the relationship between myth and history in India, which is to say that the Hindu sets more store by myth than by history. A. Berriedale Keith observed in 1920:

Nor were the Indians without what seemed to them an excellent substitute for history in our sense. To the average Indian now, and doubtless of centuries ago, the heroes of the past and those historical kings who had been converted by their imagination into heroic figures were quite as real as, if not more real than, their local princes of the present time. Nor was it merely that they were as real; they possessed the great advantage of being recognized and admired over wide areas of India. It is hardly wonderful, therefore, that even those chronicles and panegyrics which were composed in honour of contemporary princes were soon no longer copied by scribes or studied, preference being accorded in lieu to works like the epics, which were certain to be of abiding interest. It has been well remarked that, while the Pandits have copied and commented with eagerness on the *Naiṣadhīya* of Śriharṣa, they have allowed to sink into oblivion the *Navasāhasāṅkacarita*, which he wrote to celebrate the deeds of his patron.[29]

The point can involve some subtlety—that history may not have to be divorced from myth as in the West, but may coexist with it. This would be one way of interpreting such works as the Rāmacarita of Sandhyākara (12th century) 'which can be read as applying either to the legendary Rāma of Ayodhyā or to the historical king Rāmapāla of Bengal, who was the poet's contemporary and patron'.[30] To the same genre belongs the 'Navasāhasāṅkacarita of Padmagupta, also called Parimala, whose work, in eighteen cantos, was written about 1005. It relates the mythical theme of the winning of the princess Çaçiprabhā, but is intended at the same time to allude to the history of king Sindhurāja Navasāhasāṅka of Mālava; we have by the hand of Bilhaṇa a similar example of this curious treatment in the drama *Karṇasundarī* in which he celebrates, under the guise of the marriage of a Caulukya prince to the daughter of a Vidyādhara king, an actual wedding of his patron to a princess.'[31]

Such treatments might appear far-fetched to a modern reader, but the vital linking of myth to history in the Hindu context is something which historians might ignore only at the risk of failing to understand even modern history. Sheldon Pollock notes in the context of the Rāmajanmabhūmi movement:

> Initially, I was interested only to discover when, in what circumstances, and with what significations the Rāmāyaṇa entered the arena of political discourse in South Asia, to become a language in which the political imagination expresses itself. But the materials and the historical specificity they reveal become intriguing in their own right. They also raised questions that were larger and more puzzling, questions for cultural theory generally and for our theorization of forms of Indian culture, and to some extent even for the self-understanding and sense of purpose of critical-historical Indian studies.
>
> One of these questions is the problem of what may be termed historical imagination. What concerns me under this rubric is why and how it is that people seem to bring to consciousness or even enact world-historical events only or especially through a revivification of a cultural past; why 'revolution,' in the sense of profound

and sudden social-political change, is often conceptualized by its agents as a kind of repetition. A second and more specific question relates to the Rāmāyaṇa narrative itself. Can we identify any conceptual or imaginative resources it may provide that made this narrative in particular the representational instrument of choice for figuring forth the historical events that are at issue here? More difficult still is the question of what, if anything, this evidence suggests for our understanding of the modalities of relations between communities in western and central India in the eleventh to fourteenth centuries. Finally, since all historical work is informed by, if not an argument about, the present, what difference does knowing this past make in comprehending the present-day redeployment of Rāmāyaṇa symbology, let alone in addressing the current crisis? What critical value can attach to historiography, and what are the possibilities of historicist intervention in the social-political world of the present, especially given the role of objectivist history in creating the world? In short, why should we want any longer to be historical?

In answer to these questions he offers a historical study of the mythos of Rāmāyaṇa:

I suggest in what follows that the Rāmāyaṇa came alive in the realm of public political discourse in western and central India in the eleventh to fourteenth centuries in a dramatic and unparalleled way. I believe the text offers unique imaginative instruments—in fact, two linked instruments—whereby, on the one hand, a divine political order can be conceptualized, narrated, and historically grounded, and, on the other, a fully demonized Other can be categorized, counterposed, and condemned. The makers of elite culture in medieval South Asia chose these instruments for the work of divinization and demonization at this historical moment because of the emergence of two enabling conditions. One was the peculiar salience that a far older political theology now seems to have achieved in the service of the legitimation or enhancement or perhaps just self-understanding of kingship. The other was the appearance of Others who—whether, in fact, they presented an unprecedented unassimilability or could opportunistically be represented as such—were especially vulnerable to the demonizing formulation the Rāmāyaṇa made available. All this I feel reasonably confident in arguing. What remains far less easy to figure out is how this material is to be interpreted in understanding community interaction and what pertinence this kind of genealogy has with respect to the problems of the present. The proper and critical task of history here may not be what 'really happened' but how people come to believe what happened. The symbolic meaning system of a political culture is constructed, and perhaps knowing the processes of construction is a way to control it.[32]

Kees W. Bolle probes this 'deep structure' connecting myth and history in Hinduism at another level. He claims that 'the suggestion that a real myth cannot be related to specific happenings is open to severe doubt' and in support he adduces the following evidence:

Of the kingdom of Fu-nan, flourishing from about the first century AD to the seventh century AD with its center in the Mekong delta in Southeast Asia, a curious legend was recorded. According to it, the Kingdom owed its origin to the marriage of an Indian, the first king of the land, and the local queen. In much later times, at the court of Angkor, a union of the same type was still commemorated. It is one of the most splendid examples of a founding myth, yet there is no doubt that it expresses the historical fact of Southeast Asia's Hinduization, the alliance of Indian and local creativity. True myth and reminiscence of history are not mutually exclusive. A Samoyed tribal myth shows this point even more emphatically. We know the history of the Russians who brought Siberia under their sway. The Samoyed myth tells about a struggle between two parties: the tribal community represented by their cultural hero Itje, and the alliance of Satan and Jesus Christ, who is called the 'father of all Russians'. The 'evil powers' became the masters of the land. Itje left his people but promised to return to gather his tribe together and drive out the foreigners. Obviously this is a real myth, one of some primitive Messianism. But it is equally obvious how it grew up on historical fact. Finally, it must be said that de Vries' work in his own field of specialization suggests that his remarks should not be understood as a summary dismissal of the possibility of myths with historical origins.[33]

This fusion of the historical and mythical horizons at a more philosophical level is also apparent in the following remarks of N. A. Nikam:

What is history but a 'regressive' perspective of time; and, every culture has a sense of history; every culture has its 'golden age' and a memory of the deeds of its heroes, and has its tradition. But as a regress into the past is always possible so there is 'history' behind history, and so the paradox of history is that in human culture the beginnings of history are not in history but in 'pre-history', and pre-history merges into the myth. Indian Culture, Hinduism in particular, is the forgotten memory of the beginninglessness of an undated tradition sanātana dharma alive to look back upon its own past in order to live in a changing future. 'Everything depends upon the past and a revolution at the same time; the re-entrance into tradition but a tradition which has been transformed.' This is what Indian Culture, and Hinduism in particular, aim to be. Nature and history are both concerned with time but while nature is the realm of what 'happens', history is the realm of what man 'makes', but man makes history only when he makes *new* history and does not repeat history, and so, history is not merely memory but hope. In Indian Culture, history is both memory and hope; but hope is greater than memory; says the *Chāndogya Upaniṣad: āśā vā va smarād bhūyasī*, 'Hope, assuredly, is greater than memory' (VII.14.1). In the same passage it says: 'When kindled by hope, memory learns the sacred hymns, performs sacrifices, desires sons and cattle, desires this world and the other.' The classical tradition in Indian Culture is to 'desire this world and the other;' Indian Culture says that man makes history when 'he saves himself by himself and does not destroy himself', *uddharet ātmanā ātmanaṁ, na ātmanaṁ avasādayet*; the history of the world lies in the history of man, in his actions; whereas Sartre says in his *Existentialism and Humanism* 'We should act without hope', the philosophy of Indian Culture believes in the opposite paradox that action itself is hope.[34]

(10) This 'problem' of the absence of a sense of history has sometimes also evoked a philosophical response. A. Berriedale Keith writes:

Something too must be allowed for the tendency of the Indian mind to prefer the general to the particular, which is shown in widely different spheres of knowledge. We hear, for instance, in Buddhist texts of certain definite heresies, but we are equally faced with schematic lists of unsound philosophical views which are asserted to have been held by others, but which in large measure are obviously mere inventions. Throughout the history of Indian philosophy the same thing is seen; no one seems to be in the least interested in the history of doctrines, no one writes a history of philosophy as contrasted with summaries of opposing doctrines; no one even attempts a real history of politics or medicine. What interests writers is not questions of the opinions of predecessors as individuals, but the discussion of divergencies of doctrine all imagined as having arisen *ex initio*. The names of some great authorities may be preserved, as in the case of the schools of philosophy, but nothing whatever with any taint of actuality is recorded regarding their personalities, and we are left to grope for dates. This indifference to chronology is seen everywhere in India, and must be definitely connected, in the ultimate issue, with the quite secondary character ascribed to time by the philosophies.[35]

Thus Keith would have one connect Hindu concepts of history with the Hindu concepts of time. Scholars are however divided on this point. Some are of the view that the vast spans of time in Hindu cosmology dwarf historical time but others are of the view that these computations are so vast that they self-destruct, leaving the field clear for the concept of historical time.[36]

(11) Sometimes the philosophical response has consisted in trying to explain this absence of a sense of history among the Hindus in terms of Hindu philosophical concepts such as that of Karma. Thus A. Berriedale Keith writes:

From the standpoint of psychology it is not difficult to understand that the view that history had any meaning or value was one unlikely to receive acceptance in India. The prevailing doctrines told distinctly against any such estimate of event. In the strict logical sense of the doctrine of Karman all men's actions were the outcome of actions done in previous births; they were, therefore, wholly incalculable, for no one could tell what deed in the remotest past might not spring up to work out its inevitable end. Beside this belief, and evidently in full strength in may minds, was the view that all things were brought about by fate, working in a manner wholly unintelligible and beyond all foresight. To these more rational views, which might be combined and even reconciled by exercise of a little ingenuity, was added the acceptance by the Indian mind of the miraculous in the shape of divine intervention, magic, and witchcraft. The scientific attitude of mind which seeks to find natural causes for events of nature is not normal in India, and the conception that nature is not capable of being affected by divine or demoniac instrumentalities would have seemed ludicrous to the vast majority of its people; Buddhists and Jains were as little inclined to abandon popular superstitions as were Brahmins. Nay, all three religions favoured the belief in the habit of sages by asceticism to attain magic powers; the doctrine that these powers can be acquired by regular forms of process is inculcated in their philosophies, and persons who were able to achieve these results were capable of affecting the processes of nature, so that to ascribe similar powers to superhuman beings was perfectly natural. Moreover, the philosophies of every kind taught that there was no progress in our sense in the world; things had happened age after age in precisely the same way; the doctrine of the periodical creation and destruction of the world of the Brahmanical post-Vedic texts is on the same plane as the theory of the Buddhists of the existence of innumerable earlier Buddhas and the long line of Jain Tīrthaṅkaras.[37]

This view then seems to find further support in the fact that: 'A history of Indian philosophy was never attempted in India; the most that was achieved was the grouping of systems by reason of their similarities, and accounts of contending views based on the desire to prove by this means the superiority of some doctrine or other.'[38]

Such a view, while it might account for a lack of historical sense induced during certain periods of Hinduism in terms of the trials to which it was subjected by history, is hard to reconcile with the historical details available from other periods. For instance, the Manusmṛti (IX.301) maintains that the king is the maker of the Age, rather than vice versa as Keith seems to imply. Nor is it entirely clear that belief in predestination must produce inertia. It has been pointed out, for instance, that the 'Protestant ethic'—a phrase made famous by Max Weber—'was linked to the belief that God predestined some to salvation and some to eternal damnation. The paradox was that belief in predestination seemed not to discourage human activity but rather to encourage it, since no one knew if he or she was not among the elect.'[39] Nor does predestination seem to be the sole or even the main line along which the doctrine of karma has been interpreted within Hinduism[40] and Yogasūtra (II.16) directly contradicts such a view, by insisting that such suffering as has not yet been experienced can be prevented.

(12) Some scholars have identified this lack of a sense of history, to the

extent that it is to be deduced from a lack of Hindu historiography, as a Brahmanical rather than a Hindu characteristic. Vincent A. Smith wrote in the 1920s:

The trite observation that Indian literature, prior to the Muhammadan period, does not include formal histories, although true in a sense, does not present the whole truth. Most of the Sanskrit books were composed by Brahmans, who certainly had not a taste for writing histories, their interest being engaged in other pursuits. But the Rajas were eager to preserve annals of their own doings, and took much pains to secure ample and permanent record of their achievements. They are not to blame for the melancholy fact that their efforts have had little success. The records laboriously prepared and regularly maintained have perished almost completely in consequence of the climate, including insect pests in that term, and of the innumerable political revolutions from which India has suffered. Every court in the old Hindu kingdoms maintained official bards and chroniclers whose duty it was to record and keep up the annals of the state.

He goes on to say:

Some portion of such chronicles has been preserved and published by Colonel Tod, the author of the famous book, *Annals and Antiquities of Rajasthan*, first published in 1829, but that work stands almost alone. The great mass of the Rajas' annals has perished beyond recall. Some fragments of the early chronicles clearly are preserved in the royal genealogies and connected historical observations recorded in the more ancient Purāṇas; and numerous extracts from local records are given in the prefaces to many inscriptions. Thus it appears that the Hindus were not indifferent to history, although the Brahmans, the principal literary class, cared little for historical composition as a form of literature, except in the form of *praśastis*, some of which are poems of considerable literary merit. Such Sanskrit histories as exist usually were produced in the border countries, the best being the metrical chronicle of Kashmir, called the *Rāja-taraṅgiṇī*, composed in the twelfth century. Even that work does not attain exactly to the European ideal of a formal history. Several Brahman authors, notably Bāṇa in the seventh century, wrote interesting works, half history and half romance, which contain a good deal of authentic historical matter. Our exceptionally full knowledge of the story of Harshavardhana, King of Thānēsar and Kanauj, is derived largely from the work of Bāṇa entitled 'The Deeds of Harsha'.

Historical or semi-historical compositions are numerous in the languages of the south. The Mackenzie collection of manuscripts catalogued by H. H. Wilson contains a large number of texts, which may be regarded as histories in some degree.[41]

He also adds in a footnote: 'The survey of Rājputāna literature now in progress will disclose many more historical works.'[42]

A. A. Macdonell anticipates Smith by a decade or more. He already wrote in 1900 that 'History is the one weak spot in Indian literature' and that 'two causes seem to have combined to bring about this remarkable result', namely,

> In the first place, early India wrote no history because it never made any. The ancient Indians never went through a struggle for life, like the Greeks in the Persian and the Romans in the Punic wars, such as would have welded their tribes into a nation and developed political greatness. Secondly, the Brahmans, whose task it would naturally have been to record great deeds, had early embraced the doctrine that all action and existence are a positive evil, and could therefore have felt but little inclination to chronicle historical events.[43]

Here we are concerned with Macdonell's second reason, which has not gone unchallenged. Troy Wilson Organ objects to the remark by A. A. Macdonell that ' ... the Brahmans, whose task it would naturally have been to record great deeds, had early embraced the doctrine that all action and existence are a positive evil, and could therefore have felt but little inclination to chronicle historical events.' According to Organ such a view

> is true, but misleading. The belief that 'all action and existence are a positive evil' was not always a belief of the Brahmins. Not enough recognition has been given to the fact that Hindus are great storytellers, and that their history is embodied largely in legends, fairy tales, and myths. This is not history, as it is commonly known. No records were kept as they were in China. What the Hindus felt worth preserving was the meaning of events, not a record of when the events took place. They were a tradition-minded, but not a history-minded, people. This is still largely true.
>
> ... Indian history was first written by Westerners to understand the land and people over which they ruled. Such histories attempted to fit Indian history into a typical Western mold of Ancient, Medieval, and Modern—Modern begins with the British occupation!—and they also showed India as a nation molded by a series of foreign invasions, neglecting to report her continuous cultural and political background.[44]

According to this line of response *tradition* does duty for history for the Hindu, and this tradition was maintained by the Brahmins, so both the idea and the explanation that Hindus lack a sense of history because the Brahmins lacked an interest in it, may have to be revisited. Prakash N. Desai has such a 'tradition' in mind when he writes:

> This typology tells us how Indians use history. What it does not explicitly convey is the intense Hindu preoccupation with the past. *Itihās*, 'it happened thus', is intimately relevant to how we do things now. For a Hindu, it is not that 'those who forget their history are bound to repeat it'; the Hindu ethos demands that you remember your history and insists that you repeat it. Thus, when Hindus glow with pride

declaring that theirs is an ancient civilization, the emotion is sincere and profound. They speak of their ancestors of centuries past with a feeling of immediacy and carry the name of their *gotra*, the lineage which dictates specific transactions and forbids others. These forefathers are enshrined in the collective memory through daily observances and are celebrated as the founders of a great tradition. What the heroes of Hindu faith have taught, contemporary Hindus insist, has helped preserve the tradition in its pristine form.

For Hindus, history is a lived-in reality. The survival of major treatises for centuries, written down perhaps only after the development of the Brahmi script (considered to have been finished in about 300 BCE) attests to the emphasis placed on memory—remembering the past and interpreting it to serve the present. This gives to the Hindu culture both a paleocentric and mythopoetic character.

Such tradition involves a certain reverence for the past:

Hindus revere the past, but not only in a religious sense; the past is looked to also for inspiration and prescription of social and personal conduct. The ancient Vedic literature, the later epics, and the medieval tales of the past (*purāṇas*) illustrate through the mythmaking the essential relationships between humans and institutions. Whether in a family or a classroom, in politics or the workplace, ancient heroes and their deeds are recalled, and the present compared with the past. In the process, old myths change and new ones are generated. Unknown facts are filled in, and the accounts become richer as they pass from mouth to mouth and generation to generation. As every Indian will say, 'Don't confuse me with facts; the ones I don't know, I will make up.' To complete stories and leave no loose threads is an art form; this can be clearly seen in Indian cinema, where little is left implicit.

This attitude has resulted in flexible rules of ethical and moral conduct. Although Hindus recall their early past to guide them in their actions, the narrative of the conduct of their ancestors are given new forms, and stories are adapted to the needs of the present. Different versions of ancient text exist, and different texts always tell slightly altered accounts of particular events. This constant accommodation gives the Hindus their amazing diversity yet keeps them in the fold.[45]

(13) Some have tried to explain the absence of a sense of history in terms of want of national feeling, thereby finding a political explanation for the historical problem. A. A. Macdonell hints at this, as noted earlier, when he writes:

Early India wrote no history because it never made any. The ancient Indians never went through a struggle for life, like the Greeks in the Persian and the Romans in the Punic wars, such as would have welded their tribes into a nation and developed political greatness.[46]

A. Berriedale Keith develops the point further as follows:

It may be admitted that the foreign attacks on India in the period of the first four centuries BC were probably not such as to excite deep national feeling. Alexander's invasion was followed by the early loss of the most Indian of the territories won to Candragupta, apparently without any such struggle as would induce a sense of national danger and national triumph. The Greek, Parthian, Çaka, and Kuṣaṇa [*sic*] successes were possible in large measure because such a sentiment did not exist, and the process of assimilation went on so steadily that, when the Gupta revival came, it can hardly have been felt as a national revival, however much it seems so to us *ex post facto*. Thereafter, until the eleventh century, the wars of India were merely struggles between rival dynasties, wars of crows and kites, in which no deep signification could lie. The Mahomedan invaders found India without any real national feeling; their successes were rendered possible largely because the chiefs disliked one another far more than they did the Mleccha. It is characteristic that even in the ballads evoked by the struggle the sense of nationality is only in process of development.[47]

The view that ancient Indians lacked political feeling uniformly, however, has been contested by such historians as H. C. Raychaudhuri.[48]

(14) Sometimes it has been argued that while the Hindus may or may not have had a sense of history, they did possess a sense of antiquity. A. L. Basham remarks, for instance, that 'the earliest Europeans to visit India found a culture fully conscious of its own antiquity—a culture which indeed exaggerated that antiquity, and claimed not to have fundamentally changed for many thousands of years.'[49] M. Winternitz accounts for this claim somewhat differently:

Whatever seems good, true and right, to the Indian, that he raises to the greatest possible age; and if he wants to impart a special sanctity to any doctrine, or if he wishes that his work shall be as widespread as possible, and gain respect, then he veils his name in a modest incognito, and mentions some ancient sage as the author of the book. This still happens at the present day, and in past centuries it was no different. It is for this reason that so many quite modern works pass under the time-honoured name of 'Upaniṣads' or 'Purāṇas,' new, sour wine put into old bottles. The intention to deceive, however, is as a rule out of the question in these cases. It is only that extreme indifference reigns with regard to the right of literary ownership and the desire of asserting it. Only in the later centuries does it happen that authors give their own names with full details, together with the names of their parents, grandparents, teachers, patrons, and scanty biographical note about themselves.[50]

Some have argued that this charge of a lack of historical sense applies only to Vedic literature in India, and the point is sustained paradoxically in a strictly historical and a highly theological manner. Thus Pargiter maintains that Vedic literature is wanting in 'the historical sense' and therefore 'should not always be trusted.'[51] (In this he is challenged by Keith, however, who 'disbelieves the historicity of any event not explicitly mentioned in the Vedas'.)[52]

The Hindu school of philosophy known as Mīmāṁsā similarly argues for its own 'theological' reasons, that the Vedas do not contain references to specific historical events (for this would compromise their universality and eternality). As is well known, 'according to the Mīmāṁsā, no history and certainly no factual empirical knowledge can be had from the Veda; because in the eternal book, which is prior to all individual persons and things, there cannot be any reference to persons and places.'[53] The exegetical method of Mīmāṁsā in this context may be illustrated with the help of the following examples:

> An example would serve to show the Mīmāṁsā method: A passage in the *Taittirīya Saṁhitā* says, 'Prajāpati (the creator) drew out his own omentum, and placed it in fire; from it the goat arose, and it is thus that people get cattle'. Śabara explains this passage thus: 'Prajāpati' must be an eternal object: wind, sky, or sun. 'It drew out its omentum' means it gave forth rain, wind or rays (respectively). The 'fire' in which it was thrown was either lightning or ordinary fire. 'Goat' means food, seed, or creeper, by using which men get cattle. Thus all these words are metonyms (*gauṇa*).
>
> Vedic passages such as 'Bound by the gods, fire cried and its tears become silver' have no sense of their own; they are to be taken as meant for extolling or condemning a certain action; for instance, in this case it is meant to bring home the unsuitability of that worthless metal (silver) as a sacrificial gift.[54]

The following remarks of K. Satchidananda Murty now become relevant from the point of view of the present discussion.

> Similarly, Kumārila tells us, the numerous stories about creation and destruction, the rise and fall of nations, which are to be found in the Purāṇas etc., are not factual; but they are only intended to teach some maxim such as that 'The gross comes from the subtle', 'Earthly goods are impermanent', or 'Destiny is stronger than human efforts'.
>
> Though the Mīmāṁsā holds that there are gods to whom offerings are made in sacrifices, it maintains that these 'gods' are not persons with bodies. Statements such as 'Indra killed Vṛtra', found in the Veda, cannot prove that Indra was a person with a physical body, because this sentence is an *arthavāda*, and has no independent significance. Nor are 'gods' the bestowers of fruits, for by their own potency actions enable the agent to obtain the proper fruits. Āpadeva, a popular Mīmāṁsā writer, says that 'gods' have no existence apart from the *mantras*; a 'god' is only a name inflected in the dative case in formulae (*mantras*) uttered while offering oblations.[55]

This attitude of 'demythologizing the Vedas' is not restricted to the Mīmāṁsā. For instance, 'the *Mahābhārata* indicates that the Vṛtra legend and the sacrificial acts can be understood symbolically. If Vṛtra is tamas, ignorance, Indra's vajra is viveka, discrimination, as Nīlakaṇṭha explained.'[56]

It is perhaps worth adding that this is not the only attitude found within the tradition. Yāska (fifth century BC) testifies to a school of Vedic interpretation, which was inclined to take Vedas 'historically'.[57] In the same spirit it must also be added that Mīmāṁsā had its own ahistorical way of even interpreting *smṛti* material. To cite only two examples, 'Kumārila Bhaṭṭa explains the seduction of Ahalyā as Indra's (the sun's) carrying away the shades of night, Ahalyā signifying night.'[58] Similarly, he tries to exegete away the apparently polyandrous marriage of Draupadī with the five Pāṇḍava brothers: 'Kumārilabhaṭṭa in his Tantravārtika cuts this Gordian knot by putting forward three explanations, one of which boldly asserts that there were many Draupadīs very similar to each other and so the epic figuratively speaks to one Draupadī only. There were really five Draupadīs (and not one) married separately to the five Pāṇḍavas.'[59]

(15) Another approach suggests a new perspective on the question of Hinduism and its relation to history. To follow this approach one must begin by asking two fundamental questions: what do we mean by Hinduism and what do we mean by history? Hinduism can mean many things. In this section we shall refer to only one aspect of Hinduism—that represented by the Viśiṣṭādvaita tradition, especially as articulated by Rāmānuja and his successors.

History too can mean many things; in the context of religion its two main senses have been historiographic and theological. Thus when it is alleged that Hindus have no sense of history what is often meant is that they hardly ever wrote about the historical vicissitudes, especially in a chronologically consistent way. This is the historiographic sense of the word. Then there is the theological sense of the word, as when it is said that the Western religions have a sense of history—in the sense of God acting in history, of God intervening in history and influencing history.[60] The word history is used in this latter sense in this section.

Before we get to the question of history itself, however, we have to talk about other things. For the purpose of this section this detour is a shortcut. One starts out by recognizing that in the system of Viśiṣṭādvaita Vedānta one speaks of the three basic categories called *tattva-traya*. These are Īśvara, Cit, and Acit or God, soul, and matter.[61] These Sanskrit words, however, can as well be translated as God, Man, and Nature. The change of terminology also induces a change in perspective. We are now able to perceive a degree of correspondence between Viśiṣṭādvaitic theology and Christian theology at the level of fundamental philosophical categorization.

Christian theology in particular and the whole Judeo-Christian tradition in general, however, does not stop here—it has a fourth key category which it calls history. And then one is told that this is what sets the Western religions of Judaism and Christianity apart from Hinduism. It was pointed out earlier, however, that this theological notion of history involves the intervention of God in such a way as to affect the destiny of man. And Hinduism, we have been repeatedly told, has no such sense of history.

Is it true, it must now be asked, that Hinduism possesses no such sense of history? In the Western acceptance, it is God who takes the initiative in this intervention. In order then to find a parallel to such a notion of history, if it exists, one should examine the category of *avatāra* or incarnation in Hinduism more closely. Such an examination reveals that Viśiṣṭādvaita Vedānta acknowledges five forms of God, one of which is *vibhava*. These 'incarnated (*vibhava*) forms of Viṣṇu are the Avatāras'[62] or Incarnations.

The concept of an *avatāra* clearly implies the idea of God's intervention in history. In Judaism, God's intervention is personal, in the sense that God is personally involved in the fate of his people; it is not personal in the sense that God himself personally descends among them.[63] In Christianity, however, God is incarnated as man—as full man (and full God).[64] But such an incarnation occurred only once—this is where a difference emerges on the question of God's incarnatory intervention in history within Christianity and Hinduism.[65]

It is clear, therefore, that at least in the form of Hinduism represented by Śrī Vaiṣṇavism there is a clear concept of God's intervention in history. To be sure it is not identical with that in Christianity.[66] But while they may not be twins, can there be any doubt that they belong to the same family?

(16) Yet another response has been to say that Hinduism has history but of a different or alternative kind. This is the position taken by Ashis Nandy.[67] His position is summarized by Prakash N. Desai as follows:

> Ashis Nandy, a scholar expert in political and cultural psychology, argues that the Indian culture was not ahistorical but approached history via three mediators. The first group was the minstrels, or *charans*. Wandering individually or in groups, they sang of past events or of the heroic acts of men, 'giving meaning to the present by projecting its rough realities into a mythologized past.' The second group of mediators

was genealogists and chroniclers, who constructed 'formal generational continuity.' The third were the court historians, who created 'larger-than-life subjects out of the mortals who were their masters and patrons.' All three approaches were 'deeply embedded in an orientation to the past, which reduces or elevates each social reality to a psychologically significant myth.'[68]

These three attitudes may be elaborated in Ashis Nandy's own words as follows. One attitude is represented by the *charans*:

The first attitude is that of the traditional minstrels or *charans*. These wandering individuals or small nomadic troupes who sang of past events and men—giving meaning to the present by projecting its rough realities into a mythologized past so that the present became more 'liveable'. Moving from village to village, singing of things the villagers would never live with but were expected to live by, they made history a folk art—a shared phantasy, if you like. While providing a capsulated world image and organized ethical criteria to the laity, they built a defensive shield which consolidated the culture through constant affirmation and renewal of its psycho-philosophical base.[69]

A second attitude is represented by the Barots:

The second attitude is that of the Brahminic barots who were genealogists and chroniclers. Using the legitimacy traditionally given to 'pure data' uncoloured by emotions, they communicated a sense of formal generational continuity by ignoring individuals of flesh and blood. No sanctity, however, attached to the totality of the facts. It was through selective presentation of facts, including a huge load of trivia, that the genealogist made his point. His very affectlessness came handy in this; he used it to rectify all human relationships and make history an impersonal, dehumanized, abstract, tireless 'mathematics'.[70]

A third attitude is represented by court historians:

Thirdly, there were the court historians and their humbler versions, the bhats, who sang praises of their royal employers. The attitude of court historians, however, could be independent of both the court historians and their royal patrons, and others too created mythical larger-than-life subjects out of the mortals who happened to be the objects of their interest. Everyone, including the subjects of praise, knew this to be a game and nobody took the content of the praise seriously. It was only the form of praise that was ritually important.

All three attitudes were deeply embedded in an orientation to the past which reduces—or elevates—each social reality to a psychologically significant myth. The aim is to wipe out the historical reality altogether or supplant it by the structural realities of the mythical. It is then, from the second set of realities, that the 'secondary' historicized facts of a man's life are deduced.[71]

(17) Some have taken the view that the notion that India has no history is like saying that an old man, because he now looks old, never had a youth. In other words, the impression that India has no history is not a sign that India suffers from '*arrested* growth' but rather from '*terminated* growth'—such a termination as the West itself might well experience if the lessons of the past are not heeded.[72] According to Amaury de Riencourt, Europeans committed two errors in their intellectual approach to India when they came in contact with it. On the one hand, they were unwilling to look for a comprehensive and objective philosophy of history which might determine the great similarities between the historical evolutions of India and the West—and of all civilizations, for that matter. They were thus unable to determine at what stage of their evolutions both India and the West had arrived.

Yet it was obvious that an India that was old when Alexander the Great invaded its fringe had already gone through the same stages of cultural development through which the West itself was proceeding two thousand years later and in the same sequence. On the other hand, the Europeans felt more or less unwilling to see the unique, original and utterly incompatible features of Indian civilization. Some Westerners, repelled by the more gruesome aspects of Hinduism, saw in India only a conglomeration of Pagan sects—addicted to the most barbaric customs; others, with a more or less pseudo-mythical bent, saw in India the land of eternal wisdom and the fount of a world-wide spiritual revival of the future.[73]

Amaury de Riencourt then proceeds to conclude as follows:

From this initial misreading of the past sprang all the other misconceptions. A great myth arose among Westerners watching the ocean-like uniformity of a static Indian civilization which never seemed to be stirred by the slightest breeze, whereas dynamic Europe was perpetually in the throes of convulsions—the myth of the 'timeless East', a sluggish giant who was forever condemned to follow clumsily in the wake of Western progress. What the West failed to understand was that India, as well as China had long since passed the point at which Europe and America were arriving in the nineteenth century.[74]

(18) Another interesting response to the alleged lack of a sense of history on the part of the Hindus is provided by Pandit J. L. Nehru. Pandit Nehru mediates this response by connecting a lack of sense of *history* with the absence of a sense of *factity*. He writes:

This lack of historical sense did not affect the masses, for as elsewhere, and more so than elsewhere, they built up their view of the past from the traditional accounts and myth and story that were handed to them from generation to generation. This imagined history and mixture of fact and legend became widely known and gave to the people a strong and abiding cultural background. But the ignoring of history had evil consequences, which pursue us still. It produced a vagueness of outlook, a divorce from life, as it is, credulity, a woolliness of the mind where fact was concerned. That mind was not at all woolly in the far more difficult but inevitably vaguer and more indefinite realms of philosophy; it was both analytic and synthetic, often very critical, sometimes skeptical. But where fact was concerned, it was uncritical, perhaps because it did not attach much importance to fact as such.[75]

Nehru then connects this with a Hindu predisposition to emotion rather than reason, and although recognizing that contact with science and the modern world has promoted a sense of rationality, nevertheless notes that 'even today it is strange how we suddenly become overwhelmed by tradition and the critical faculties of even intelligent men cease to function. This may partly be due to the nationalism that consumes us in our present state. Only when we are politically and economically free will the mind function normally and critically.'[76]

Around the time he was writing his book, India was in the midst of celebrating the completion of two thousand years of the calendar of Vikram Samvat, in April 1944. He noticed the contradiction between the lack of solid factual support for the fact that the era was founded by Vikrama,[77] and the emotional enthusiasm with which it was being celebrated. Here again he thought that current nationalism had a role in it, for he found 'interesting ... how emphasis is laid on his fight against the foreigner and his desire to establish the unity of India under one national state'[78] (although in fact his realm was 'confined to north and central India').[79]

Nehru, however, feels the need to justify such Hindu nationalism by pairing it off with British imperialism. For he goes on to say:

It is not Indians only who are affected by nationalist urges and supposed national interest in the writing or consideration of history. Every nation and people seem to be affected by this desire to gild and better the past and distort it to their advantage. The histories of India that most of us have had to read, chiefly written by Englishmen, are usually long apologies for and panegyrics of British rule and a barely veiled contemptuous account of what happened here in the millennia preceding it. Indeed real history, for them, begins with the advent of the Englishmen into India; all that went before is in some mystic kind of way a preparation for this divine consummation. Even the British period is distorted with the object of glorifying British rule and British virtues. Very slowly a more correct perspective is developing. But we need not go to the past to find instances of the manipulation of history to suit particular ends and support one's own fancies and prejudices. The present is full of this, and if the present, which we have ourselves seen and experienced, can be so distorted, what of the past?

Nevertheless, it is true that Indians are peculiarly liable to accept tradition and report it as history, uncritically and without sufficient examination. They will have to rid themselves of this loose thinking and easy way of arriving at conclusions.[80]

These curious and slightly convoluted comments are revealing in their own way. First, a link is forged between a lack of historical sense with the world of emotions. Then, while such emotionalism in general is considered suspect, it is acceptable when it assumes the form of Indian nationalism, specially when it is presented as a foil to British imperialism. Nevertheless the hope is expressed that Indians will become more scientific, presumably once they are free (this last point providing an interesting subscript). Nehru does not say so but one could extrapolate that once they are free they will also be able to write their own history, since he earlier quotes a British author to the effect that 'our writing of India's history is perhaps resented more than anything else we have done'.[81]

Similar wonder then that within two decades of India's independence one witnessed the launching of the 'History and Culture of the Indian People' project, launched by the Bharatiya Vidya Bhavan. Its first volume, entitled *The Vedic Age*, appeared in 1951 and the final volume, entitled *The Struggle for Independence*, in 1969. It is a history of India by the Indians for the Indians—and anyone else who might care to read it.[82]

These examples represent a cross section of the responses evoked among Hindus and scholars of Hinduism by the proposition that the Hindus lacked a sense of history. Most of those who offered these remarks and responses took the statement that Hindus lacked a sense of history at its face value and did not pause to consider whether the statement itself represented the reality it sought to describe correctly and adequately. The time has perhaps now come to subject the statement to such an examination.

End Notes

1. K. M. Panikkar, *The Foundations of New India* (London: George Allen & Unwin Ltd., 1968), p. 68.
2. Ibid., pp. 68–9
3. Ibid., p. 69.
4. Max Müller, *India: What Can It Teach Us?* (London: Longmans, Green, & Co., 1899), p. 63.

5. See Ronald B. Inden, *Imagining India* (Bloomington and Indianapolis: Indiana University Press, 2000 [1990]), *passim*.

6. See Radha Kumud Mookerji, *Glimpses of Ancient India* (Bombay: Bharatiya Vidya Bhavan, 1961), Chapter XIII.

7. R. C. Majumdar, 'Sources of Indian History', in R. C. Majumdar, ed., *The Vedic Age* (London: George Allen & Unwin Ltd., 1952), pp. 47–8.

8. Ibid., pp. 49–50.

9. Madhav Deshpande, 'History, Change and Permanence: A Classical Indian Perspective', in Gopal Krishna, ed., *Contributions to South Asian Studies* (Delhi: Oxford University Press, 1979), p. 21.

10. Ibid., p. 21.

11. Ibid., p. 10.

12. *The Collected Works of Mahatma Gandhi* (New Delhi: Publications Division, Government of India, 1962), Vol. X, pp. 46–7.

13. B. Ganguli, *Gandhi's Social Philosophy: Perspective and Relevance* (Delhi: Vikas Publishing House, 1973), p. 115.

14. Cited, ibid., p. 114.

15. I am indebted to Robert Sadler for this argument.

16. B. Ganguli, op. cit., p. 115.

17. D. S. Sarma, *Hinduism Through the Ages* (Bombay: Bharatiya Vidya Bhavan, 1956), p. 1.

18. M. Winternitz, *A History of Indian Literature* (Calcutta: Calcutta University Press, 1927), Vol. I, p. 30.

19. Ashis Nandy, *Alternative Sciences* (New Delhi: Allied Publishers Private Limited, 1980), p. 6.

20. See Andrew Fort, *Jīvanmukti in Transformation: Embodied Liberation in Advaita and Neo-Vedānta* (Albany NY: SUNY Press, 1998).

21. Ashis Nandy, op. cit., p. 6.

22. T. S. Rukmani, *Hinduism—A Paradigm of the Centre and the Circumference* (Inaugural Address: University of Durban-Westville, 1994), pp. 12–13.

23. Arvind Sharma, *A Hindu Perspective on the Philosophy of History* (London: Macmillan, 1990), p. ix.

24. G. C. Pande, *Foundations of Indian Culture* (Delhi: Motilal Banarsidass, 1984), Vol. I, p. 23.

25. Ainslie T. Embree, ed., *The Hindu Tradition* (New York: Random House, 1972), p. 208.

26. Ibid., pp. 220–1.

27. David Shulman, 'Reconsidering Hinduism: What I might have said (In parts if ...)', in Günther D. Sontheimer and Hermann Kulke, eds, *Hinduism Reconsidered* (Delhi: Manohar, 1989), p. 9.

28. Ibid.

29. A. Berriedale Keith, *A History of Sanskrit Literature* (London: Oxford University Press, 1920), pp. 146–7.

30. A. L. Basham, *The Wonder that was India* (New Delhi: Rupa & Co., 1999), p. 424.

31. A. Berriedale Keith, op. cit., p. 151.

32. Sheldon Pollock, 'Rāmāyaṇa and Political Imagination in India', *The Journal of Asian Studies* 52:2: 261 (May 1993).

33. Kees W. Bolle, 'Introduction', Jan de Vries, *The Study of Religion: A Historical Approach* (New York: Harcourt, Brace & World, Inc., 1967), pp. xxi–xxii.

34. N. A. Nikam, *Some Concepts of Indian Culture: A Philosophical Interpretation* (Simla: Indian Institute of Advanced Study, 1967), pp. 10–11.

35. A. Berriedale Keith, op. cit., p. 147.

36. Michael Witzel, 'On Indian Historical Writing: The Role of Vaṃśāvalīs', *Journal of the Japanese Association for South Asian Studies*, No. II (December 1990), p. 6.

37. A. Berriedale Keith, op. cit., pp. 145–6.

38. Ibid., p. 499.

39. John L. Esposito, Darrell J. Fasching and Todd Lewis, *World Religions Today* (New York and Oxford: Oxford University Press, 2002), p. 76.

40. T. M. P. Mahadevan, *Outlines of Hinduism* (Bombay: Chetana Limited, 1971), pp. 60–1.

41. Vincent A. Smith, *The Oxford History of India From the Earliest Times to the End of 1911* (Oxford: Clarendon Press, 1923), pp. xviii–xix.

42. Ibid., p. xviii, note 1.

43. Arthur A. Macdonell, *A History of Sanskrit Literature* (London: William Heinemann, 1900), p. 11.

44. Troy Wilson Organ, *The Hindu Quest for the Perfection of Man* (Athens, Ohio: Ohio University Press, 1970), pp. 30–1.

45. Prakash N. Desai, *Health and Science in the Hindu Tradition: Continuity and Cohesion* (New York: Crossroads, 1989), p. 10.

46. A. A. Macdonell, op. cit., p. 11.

47. A. Berriedale Keith, op. cit., p. 145.

48. Hemchandra Raychaudhuri, *Political History of Ancient India with a Commentary by B.N. Mukherjee* (New Delhi: Oxford University Press, 1999), pp. 238–9, 470ff.

49. A. L. Basham, op. cit., p. 4.

50. M. Winternitz, *A History of Indian Literature* (Calcutta: University of Calcutta, 1927), p. 30.

51. U. N. Ghoshal, *Studies In Indian History and Culture* (Bombay: Orient Longmans, 1965), p. 39.

52. Ibid.

53. K. Satchidananda Murty, *Revelation and Reason in Advaita Vedānta* (Delhi: Motilal Banarsidass, 1974 [1959]), p. 217.

54. Ibid.

55. Ibid., pp. 217–18.

56. K. Satchidananda Murty, *Vedic Hermeneutics* (Delhi: Motilal Banarsidass, 1993), p. 11.

57. Vasudeva Sharana Agrawala, 'Yāska and Pāṇini', in Kalidas Bhattacharyya, ed., *The Cultural History of India* (Calcutta: The Ramakrishna Mission Institute of Culture, 1958), Vol. I, p. 294.

58. Naman Shivram Apte, *The Practical Sanskrit English Dictionary* (Delhi: Motilal Banarsidass, 1965), p. 195.

59. P. V. Kane, *History of Dharmaśāstra* (Poona: Bhandarkar Oriental Research Institute, 1974), Vol. II, Pt I (second edition), p. 555.

60. See John H. Hick, *Philosophy of Religion* (fourth edition) (Englewood Cliffs, NJ: Prentice Hall, 1990), pp. 64–7.

61. See T. M. P. Mahadevan, *Outlines of Hinduism* (Bombay: Chetana Ltd., 1960), p. 151.

62. Ibid. Also see J. B. Carmen, *The Theology of Rāmānuja: An Essay in Interreligious Understanding* (New Haven and London: Yale University Press, 1974).

63. This is an interesting point of comparison between Judaism and Śaivism as 'Śiva is not said to have incarnated himself like Viṣṇu. But nevertheless he comes to the aid of man, appears in flesh and blood in different capacities to alleviate human misery' (T. M. P. Mahadevan, op. cit., p. 36). Perhaps God appears in Śaivism more often than in Judaism but a similarity in the unwillingness to incarnate should be noted.

64. See Mircea Eliade, editor in chief, *The Encyclopedia of Religion* (New York: Macmillan Publishing Company, 1987), Vol. 14, p. 103.

65. K. M. Sen, *Hinduism* (Harmondsworth: Penguin Books Ltd., 1961), p. 73, note 1.

66. It is worth noting that Christianity accepts the doctrine of incarnation notwithstanding the theological difficulties such a belief entailed, see Willard G. Oxtoby, 'The Christian Tradition', in Willard G. Oxtoby, *World Religions: Western Traditions* (second edition) (Toronto: Oxford University Press, 2002), pp. 227ff.

67. See Ashis Nandy, *Alternative Sciences* (New Delhi: Allied Publishers Private Ltd., 1980).

68. Prakash N. Desai, op. cit., p. 9.

69. Ashis Nandy, op. cit., pp. 4–5.

70. Ibid.

71. Ibid.

72. Amaury de Riencourt, op. cit., p. xii.

73. Ibid., pp. xi–xii.

74. Ibid., p. xii.

75. J. L. Nehru, *The Discovery of India* (New York: The John Day Company, 1946), p. 93.

76. Ibid.

77. See A. L. Basham, op. cit., pp. 493–4; D. C. Sircar, *Ancient Malwa and the*

Vikramāditya Tradition (Delhi: Munshiram Manoharlal, 1969); but also see R. C. Majumdar, 'The Vikrama Saṁvat and Śakābda', in R. C. Majumdar, ed., *The Age of Imperial Unity* (Bombay: Bharatiya Vidya Bhavan, 1968), pp. 154–7.

78. J. L. Nehru, op. cit., p. 94.

79. Ibid.

80. Ibid., pp. 94–5.

81. Ibid., p. 287.

82. For an early assessment of the project, see A. L. Basham, *Studies in Indian History and Culture* (Calcutta: Sambodhi Publications Private Ltd., 1964), pp. 227ff.

Does Hinduism Lack a Sense of History? Thesis Re-examined

The preceding chapters were devoted to a consideration of the emergence of the view that the Hindus lacked a sense of history, its influence on Indian Studies, and the responses it evoked. The time has now come to ask whether the proposition itself—independent of its origin, influence, and the response it has provoked—is valid or not.

Since the thesis claims that Hindus lacked a sense of history, one must now turn to an examination of such evidence on the basis of which it could be tested. One useful way of testing a thesis is to try to examine the evidence which might point in an opposite direction. Can any evidence be adduced in support of the view that the Hindus did possess a sense of history, as against not possessing it?

I

The place to look for a historical sense, if any, among the Hindus, one would imagine, would not so much be the religious literature of the Hindus, with the Brāhmaṇas acting as its custodians and maintaining it through oral transmission. For if the Indic religions do not attach the same theological or teleological value to history as the Abrahamic religions and secular Western culture is wont to, then this is obviously not the most promising place to look for it. One should instead turn to the literature left behind by those who made history in India as elsewhere: the rulers. Now,

> The favoured medium in which the rulers of India left behind their records are inscriptions. About 90,000 inscriptions have so far been discovered in different parts

of India, out of which the largest numbers come from the Tamil-, Kannada-, and Telegu-speaking areas—about 35,000, 17,000 and 10,000 respectively. Many of these inscriptions have not yet been published. Every year new inscriptions are being discovered and studied, and our knowledge of early Indian history is being gradually widened ... . The popular belief that all important inscriptions have already been discovered, studied and utilised for the reconstruction of history is wrong ... .[1]

Whether the Hindus did or did not possess a sense of history—or geography for that matter, will then have to be determined by an examination of these inscriptions.

The importance of these inscriptions in the reconstruction of ancient Indian history has been recognized for over a century now, if not longer. Vincent A. Smith writes:

Inscriptions have been given the first place in the list because they are, on the whole, the most important and trustworthy source of our knowledge. Unfortunately, they do not at present go further back than the third century BC with certainty, although it is not unlikely that records considerably earlier may be discovered, and it is possible that a very few known documents may go back beyond the reign of Aśoka. Indian inscriptions, which usually are incised on either stone or metal, may be either official documents set forth by kings or other authorities, or records made by private persons for various purposes. Most of the inscriptions on stone either commemorate particular events or record the dedication of buildings or images. The commemorative documents range from the simple signature of a pilgrim to long and elaborate Sanskrit poems detailing the achievements of victorious kings. Such poems are called *praśasti*. The inscriptions on metal are for the most part grants of land inscribed on plates of copper. They are sometimes extremely long, especially in the south, and usually include information about the reigning king and his ancestors. Exact knowledge of the dates of events in early Hindu history, so far as it has been attained, rests chiefly on the testimony of inscriptions.[2]

He goes on to say:

Records of an exceptional kind occur occasionally. The most remarkable of such documents are the edicts of Aśoka, which in the main are sermons on *dharma*, the Law of Peity or Duty. At Ajmēr in Rājputāna and at Dhar in Central India fragments of plays have been found inscribed on stone tablets. Part of a treatise on architecture is incised on one of the towers at Chitor and a score of music for the *vīṇā*, or Indian lute, has been found in the Pudukottai State, Madras. A few of the metal inscriptions are dedications, and one very ancient document on copper, the Sohgaura plate from the Gorakhpur District, is concerned with Government storehouses.

The inscriptions, which have been catalogued and published more or less fully aggregate many thousands. The numbers in the peninsula especially are numerous.[3]

Notwithstanding this tribute, epigraphic evidence on the question of the sense of history as found among the Hindus does suffer from certain limitations. As already noted in the passage just cited, very few known documents go back beyond the reign of Aśoka, that is, beyond the third century BC. They are often dated in the regnal year of the king, and when obviously not so, the era is not specified. Moreover, their distribution over the country is not even, although the fact that they relatively abound in those areas where Islamic rule took longest to penetrate invites the proposition that they may also have suffered iconoclastic destruction, in keeping with the pattern of the relative paucity of historical material for the Hindu period available from these areas. The stylistic formalism of epigraphic commemorative literature (*stuti*) may also at times compromise factual and geographical exactitude, or even truth.[4]

Nevertheless, despite these handicaps, they remain a rich resource for assessing a sense of history among the Hindus. A review of two of such well-known inscriptions: the Junagadh Inscription of Rudradāman (c. 150 AD) and the Allahabad Pillar Inscription of Samudragupta (c. 350 AD) might be helpful in this connection.

The Junagadh inscription of Rudradāman, which 'is among the earliest dated records of ancient India, and proves that Rudradāman was reigning in AD 150',[5] records the repair of a lake called Sudarśana, which had burst under the impact of a violent storm. The first point to note is that it is dated in the year 72, thus indicating a sense of chronology, although no era is specified. It is usually taken to represent the Śaka era, which places it c. 150 AD. Then the history of the construction of the dam is mentioned: as originally constructed under the orders of Vaiśya Puṣyagupta, who was the provincial governor of the region in which the dam is located, namely Saurāṣṭra, in the time of Candragupta Maurya. These names are stated as such in the epigraph and are not being inferred. It is then recorded that the facilities were upgraded and the conduits for irrigation provided by Yavanarāja Tushāspha, the governor of the same province during the time of Aśoka. Thus the succession of the kings of the Mauryan dynasty is correctly stated. The ancestry of Rudradāman himself is specified with such precision that it has helped resolve debates: it is stated that the inscription was incised in the 52nd year, in reign of Rudradāman, son of Jayadāman, *grandson* of Chashṭana and *great-grandson* of Yaśāmotika.[6] It goes on to say that in Rudradāman's time it was seriously damaged by a storm and repaired again on Rudradāman's orders. Apart from these details, several other aspects of the inscription demand attention for the historical sense implicit in them. The inscription describes Rudradāman as resorted to by all the 'castes' and chosen as their lord to protect them (*sarva-varṇa-abhigamya-rakṣaṇārthaṁ patitve vṛtena*).[7] This has been regarded as historical evidence of the election of a king in ancient India, along with that of the election of Gopāla, the founder of the Pāla Dynasty in Bengal,[8] in the eighth century.

Another interesting aspect is provided by the claim that Rudradāman was 'the restorer of kings who had been deprived of their kingdoms' (*bhraṣṭa-rāja-pratiṣṭhāpaka*).[9] The inscription refers to Rudradāman defeating Sātakarṇi, Lord of the Deccan (*dakṣiṇāpatha-pati*) twice. The exact identity of the king remains uncertain—he has been variously identified by Rapson and B. N. Mukherjee with Vāsiṣṭhīputra Śrī Sātakarṇi, by D. R. Bhandarkar with Gautamīputra Sātakarṇi himself, and by K. Gopalachari with Śiva Śrī Sātakarṇi.[10] The crucial point is that apparently the king was reinstated in the regions thus regained by defeating the Sātavāhanas. This resonates with the three kinds of conquests specified in the *Arthaśāstra*: 'the first is conquest in which the defeated king is forced to render homage and tribute, after which he, or a member of the family is reinstated as a vassal. The second is victory in which enormous booty is demanded and large portions of enemy territory annexed. The third involves the political annihilation of the conquered kingdom and its incorporation in that of the victor.'[11]

The Sanskrit terms for these are *dharmavijaya*, *lobhavijaya*, and *asuravijaya* respectively. Apparently Rudradāman was following the *dharmavijaya* model but with a wrinkle. Since areas lost to the Sātavāhanas were being recovered, this was more like *punarvijaya*; *dharmapunarvijaya*. History is here grabbing at the coat-tails of political theory. Such a policy is recommended by Kauṭilya (vii. 161) in A*rthaśāstra*, as well as by Yājñavalkya (I. 342–3) in a text of *dharmaśāstra*, and the epigraphic confirmation it receives here and partially later, indicates a general awareness of its historicity perhaps as much as its sagacity. From the point of view of the historical sense (as distinguished from the political) of the ancient Indians, it is worth noting that this epigraphic information about Rudradāman's conquest is confirmed by an extra-Indic literary source.

In the *Geography* of Ptolemy, written about AD 140 with materials gathered a few years earlier, Ozene, i.e. Ujjayanī, capital of Avanti (west Mālwā), is mentioned as the headquarters of Tiastenes, undoubtedly a Greek corruption of the name *Chashṭana*. In the Junāgarh inscription of Rudradāman, that ruler is represented as the lord of many countries including Ākara, Avanti, Anūpa, Aparānta, Saurāshṭra and Ānarta (Dvārakā region in Saurāshṭra), which had all been conquered from Gautamīputra (c. AD 106–30), probably when Rudradāman was a Kshatrapa under his grandfather. Rudradāman further claims to have twice defeated Sātakarṇi, lord of Dakshiṇāpatha, whom he did not destroy, as he was a near relative. This Sātakarṇi seems to be no other than Gautamīputra. The closeness of relation between the two rulers is explained by the Kānheri inscription which refers to a Kārdamaka princess as the daughter of Mahākshatrapa Ru(dra) who is generally identified with Rudradāman, and as the wife of Vāsisṭhīputra Sātakarṇi, apparently a co-uterine brother of Vāsisṭhīputra Pulumāvi and a son of Gautamīputra. Rudradāman's claim to have reinstated deposed kings may have reference to the reinstatement of certain feudatories of Nahapāna, ousted by Gautamīputra Sātakarṇi.[12]

In the same inscription, Rudradāman speaks of defeating the Yaudheyas: 'Loath to submit rendered proud as they were of having manifested their titles of heroes among all Kṣatriyas.'[13] A. L. Basham notes:

> The *Mahābhārata* takes full cognisance of the existence of republican tribes in Western India, and their survival until the 5th century AD is attested by numerous coins and a few short inscriptions. Perhaps the most important western republic was that of the Yaudheyas in Northern Rājasthān, which issued numerous coins, bearing the inscription 'Victory to the Yaudheya tribe': one of their official seals has been found, with the proud legend, 'Of the Yaudheyas, who possess the magic spell of victory': and one fragmentary Yaudheya inscription survives. This mentions the chief of the tribe, whose name has unfortunately been worn away by the weathering of the stone; he has the regal title of mahārāja, but he is also called *mahāsenāpati*, or general-in-chief, and he is 'placed at the head of the Yaudheya people'.[14]

There is a widespread impression that monarchy of the hereditary type was the main form of government in ancient India. The Junagadh inscription indicates that this common view may be in need of revision in more ways than one. Here we have an elected king celebrating his martial success against a republican martial tribe! It may make much more sense to consider the texture of ancient Indian polity as weaving the strands of monarchy and republicanism, and sometimes in surprising ways, than talking of it as characterized by a seamless personal despotism.

The inscription also sheds interesting light on administrative arrangements in ancient India in at least three ways. One should note that Aśoka's governor in this region was a *Yavanarāja*. This means that 'foreigners' could find gainful employment in the Indian system of government, as the name Yavanarāja Tushāshpa 'is of Iranian origin'.[15] The Junagadh inscription confirms this while describing the way repairs were carried out in Rudradāman's time.

Shortly before AD 150-51, a terrible cyclone caused a serious breach, as a result of which the Sudarśana lake ceased to exist. When the peasants were fearing failure of the annual crops, Rudradāman sent his councillors and executive officers for the repair of the dam and the reconstruction of the lake. All the officials having been unsuccessful in the task, Pahlava Suviśākha, son of Kulaipa, was appointed governor of Ānarta and Saurāshṭra. The efforts of this Parthian official in the employment of Rudradāman were crowned with success, and the reservoir was again brought into being.[16]

It also adds to our understanding of ancient Indian administration by drawing a distinction between 'deliberative officials (*matisaciva* or *dhīsaciva*) and executive officials (*karmasaciva*). The former were councillors, while the latter approximately corresponded to high-ranking civil servants of modern times.'[17] But it is the third aspect which is the most striking as it offers an insight into the working of the king's council—a reference one finds lodged in the middle of the following comment by A. L. Basham:

In fact the council often exerted great powers. It might transact business in the king's absence, and the Aśokan inscriptions show that it might make minor decisions without consulting him. The Śaka satrap Rudradāman referred the question of rebuilding the Girnar dam to his councillors, who advised against it, so that he was forced to undertake the work against their advice, apparently at the expense of the privy purse and not of public funds. The Kashmīr Chronicle gives one case of a privy council deposing the king, and another of its vetoing the king's nomination of his successor.[18]

The date of the Junagadh inscription is also of interest from another point of view. The cyclical cosmology of the *yugas* is regularly associated with Hinduism and sometimes added as evidence that the Hindus did not develop the concept of linear history. The time when this cyclical concept[19] came into vogue is far from certain, although it seems to be placed in the early centuries of the Christian era.[20] The Junagadh inscription seems to indicate a transitional phase in its growth. It contains echoes of the cataclysmic close of a *yuga* in the expression: *yuga-nidhana- sadṛśa-parama-ghora-vegena*.[21]

Some points made pertaining to Rudradāman in the Junagadh inscription await clarification. He is said 'to have enjoyed royal fortune even when he was in his mother's womb. The exact significance of the claim, however, cannot be determined in the present state of our knowledge.'[22] We referred earlier to the different views regarding the identity of the Sātakarṇi king he twice defeated but due to 'nearness of connection' (*sambandhāvidūratā*) did not destroy him. B. N. Mukherjee favours his identification with Vāsiṣṭhīputra, as opposed to the one made with Gautamīputra by D. C. Sircar earlier, when he writes:

> This Sātakarṇi can be identified with Vāsiṣṭhīputra Sātakarṇi whose queen is referred to in an inscription at Kanheri as belonging to the family of the Kārddamaka kings and as the daughter of Mahākshatrapa Rudra (Rudradāman I). The legend of a coin-type (lion: bow and tree) attributes the title of Mahākshatrapa to Vāsiṣṭhīputra. We do not know whether he controlled, at least for some time, the existing Sātavāhana territory, and especially north-western Deccan (already annexed by Rudradāman) as a subordinate ruler. His Nanaghat inscription of the regnal year 13 describes him as Chatarapana (Khatarapana = Kshatrapāṇām, i.e., 'of the Kshatrapa family'?).[23]

Two other points of a slightly different but comparatively broader interest await further examination. One of them is Rudradāman's claim that he won the title of *mahākṣatrapa* for himself (*svayamadhigata-mahāksatrapa-nāmā*). Two converging reasons have been proposed by way of explanation: it might mean that he did not inherit the title from his father, and that this royal house might have faced a serious crisis which he weathered, thereby feeling entitled to call himself mahākṣatrapa.[24] The precise explanation eludes us at the moment.[25]

A more intriguing issue is raised by the question of the degree of his commitment to the *varṇa* order, or the 'caste system', indicated in the inscription. Ram Sharan Sharma identifies Rudradāman as 'a supporter of the varṇa society',[26] on the basis of the inscription, and elsewhere brings him closer to Manu on this point when he writes: 'In the second century inscriptions of Gautamīputra Sātakarṇi and Rudradāman emphasize the preservation of *varṇas* as one of the main royal functions. This aspect is also stressed by Manu, who is keen on avoiding *varṇasaṅkara*.'[27]

This enables one to introduce a point which will be elaborated later, as to the extent to which such descriptions are historical or conventional, for in many ways the tenor of the Junagadh inscription is different from that of Manu. In fact, according to Manu, Rudradāman would probably qualify as a 'fallen kṣatriya' on account of his 'caste'. It should not be overlooked that in medieval times even the Buddhist Pāla dynastic rulers claimed to have prevented *varṇasaṅkara*.[28]

Finally, the 'Girnar inscription of Rudradāman, dated AD 150, is the earliest surviving example of courtly Sanskrit prose.'[29] This should serve both as an observation and as a warning. As an observation it helps locate the inscription in the history of Sanskrit prose, but as such prose has a tendency to become florid, it also serves as a warning to allow for a measure of literary latitude. Thus 'when Rudradāman claims on line 15 of the Junagadh inscription to have "been wreathed with many garlands at the *svayaṃvara* of king's daughters" this, too, should be regarded as poetic hyperbole in an inscription which follows conventional poetical standards'[30] similar to the claims made by Bilhaṇa about the Cālukya King Vikramāditya VI. The statement that 'his good rule ... rid his dominions of disease, robbers, wild beasts and other pests'[31] may also, at least in part, belong here, as also the latter parts of his boast 'that he filled his treasury by means of *bali*, *śulka* and *bhāga* levied according to the śāstras and that his treasury overflowed with heaps of gold, silver, diamonds, *lapis lazuli*, and other gems'.[32] It is worth noting here that 'hopeless exaggeration is less noticeable in the description of the Indian rulers of the earlier period of [Indian] history. For this reason, the earlier the king is, the greater is our reliance on his claims, in spite of the obvious fact that there is always a considerable amount of exaggeration in the royal *praśastis* composed by the court poets of Indian monarchs.'[33]

The sequel to the repairs performed on lake Sudarśana further seem to testify to a historical sense on the part of Indians. We know from the Junagadh rock inscription of Skandagupta that 'breaches again appeared in the embankment in CE 136 = 456 AD and Parṇadatta's son, Cakrapālita, who was the governor of Girnar, rebuilt it of solid masonry at an "immeasurable cost". To commemorate the successful completion of the work, a temple of the God Cakrabhrit or Viṣṇu was constructed in CE 138 = 458 AD. No traces of the lake or the temple are found now.'[34]

This takes one into the Gupta period and prepares the ground for the discussion of the Allahabad pillar inscription[35] of Samudragupta (c. 335–75).[36] The inscription 'is unhappily undated, but it is surely not a posthumous document, as supposed by Fleet. It must have been engraved about 360 AD—after the completion of Samudragupta's "digvijaya" and before the performance of *Aśvamedha* which is not mentioned in it.'[37]

As the main focus of the present disquisition is an assessment of the historical sense of the ancient Indians, and the light that epigraphic evidence might shed on the issue, the location of the inscription is worth noting. Rama Shankar Tripathi notes that 'with his ideal of war and aggrandisement, Samudragupta is the very antithesis of Aśoka, who stood for peace and piety. The former's achievements formed the subject of an elaborate panegyric by the court poet Hariṣeṇa, and, strangely enough, Samudragupta chose to leave a permanent record of his sanguinary conquests by the side of the ethical exhortations of Aśoka on one of his pillars, now inside the fort of Allahabad.'[38] If this was a deliberate decision on part of Samudragupta then it tells us a lot about the sense of history of the ancient Indians.

The two are also comparable not only graphically but also epigraphically: 'we possess a long eulogy of this king (Samudragupta) by one of his officials named Hariṣeṇa and engraved on the Aśoka pillar of Allahabad. This eulogy of *praśastis* gives a detailed account of the career and personality of Samudragupta, such as we do not possess of any other king of ancient India, except the great Maurya Emperor Aśoka.'[39]

The contents of the inscription, which seem to follow a geographical rather than a chronological order,[40] provide a clear picture of Samudragupta's pattern of military and political prowess. The pattern consists of four categories. First comes a list of nine kings who were 'violently exterminated'. One recalls here the designation of Mahāpadma Nanda as *sarvakṣatrāntaka*, or destroyer of all the *kṣatriyas*, comparable to Samudragupta's claim of being *sarvarājocchettā* (uprooter of all kings) in Āryāvarta.[41] These nine monarchs were the following: Rudradeva, Matila, Nāgadatta, Candra-varman, Gaṇapatināga, Nāgasena, Nandin, Acyuta, and Balavarman.[42] In relation to these kings Samudragupta followed the policy of *asurvijaya*, a name which, according to Hemchandra Raychaudhuri, 'may have been derived from the Assyrians, the ruthlessness of whose warfare is well known'.[43] This view is strengthened by the fact that Kauṭilya 'claims to have studied the practices prevailing in contemporary states' (II.10)[44] and although he is not contemporaneous with the Assyrians, his location at Taxila and involvement in national and (as a result of Macedonian incursion) international politics renders the idea less far-fetched than it might appear otherwise. In any case, and specially in light of the tributary (as distinguished from these annexed) states whose placement is discussed in the third category below

If we now consider the position of the tributary states on the frontiers of Samudra-gupta's dominions, we may form an idea of the territory directly under the administration of Samudra-gupta. In the east it included the whole of Bengal, excepting its south-eastern extremity. Its northern boundary ran along the foothills of the Himalayas. In the west it extended up to the territory of the Madras in the Punjāb and probably included its eastern districts between Lahore and Karnāl. From Karnāl the boundary followed the Yamunā up to its junction with the Chambal, and thence along an imaginary line drawn almost due south to Bhilsa. The southern boundary ran from Bhilsa to Jubbulpore and thence along the Vindhya range of hills. Samudra-gupta is said to have conquered all the Aṭavi-rājyas (forest kingdoms) which probably denoted the hilly tracts, full of dense forest, extending eastwards from Jubbulpore.[45]

The claim to the subjugation of forest kingdoms (*āṭavika-rājya*) of Dabhālā or the Jabalpura territory is confirmed by another inscription of Samudragupta, that at Eraṇ.[46] Similarly, the defeat of Nāgasena, one of the nine uprooted kings, is confirmed by a passage in Bāṇa's *Harṣacarita* which states that Nāgasena, born in the Nāga-family, whose confidential deliberations were divulged by a *sārikā* bird, met his doom in Padmāvatī (*nāga-kula-janmanaḥ sārikāśrāvita-manstrasya āsidnāśo nāgasenasya padmavatyām*).[47]

The second category includes rulers towards whom he followed a policy of *dharmavijaya*, or subjugation and reinstatement. He adopted this policy during his campaign in penisular India in the course of which he subdued twelve kings: Mahendra, Vyaghrarāja, Maṇṭarāja, Mahendra, Svāmidatta, Damana, Visṇugupta, Nīlarāja, Hastivarman, Ugrasena, Kubera, and Dhanañjaya.[48] The geographical location of each king is specified and suggests a march down the eastern coast to the Chera kingdom and return-march by way of Mahārāṣtra and Khandesh,[49] although four of these 'Maṇṭarāja of Kaurāla, Svāmidatta of Koṭṭūra, Nīlarāja of Avamukta and Dhanañjaya of Kusthalapura cannot be identified with certainty'.[50]

A third category consists of (nine) tribes and (five) frontier kings who submitted to the might of Samudragupta and gratified his imperial commands by 'paying all kinds of taxes, obeying his orders and coming to pay homage'.[51] Nine tribes[52] and five frontier states[53] are listed in the inscription.

These nine tribes can be divided into two groups, one group comprising the Mālavas, Yaudheyas, Madrakas, and Ārjunāyanas, which seems to lie towards the west, and another comprising the Sanakānika, Ābhīra, Prārjunas, Kākas, and Kharaparakas, which seems to lie in Central India, the identification of the last three being less certain than of the first two. Of the five frontier kingdoms, Samataṭa, Kāmarūpa, Nepāla, Ḍavāka, and Kartṛpura, the first three are well known, and the last two have been identified more tentatively with Nowgong district of Assam and Kartarpur in Jalandhar district. It is worth noting that these 'five tributary kingdoms are expressly stated to be situated on the frontiers of Samudragupta's dominions. The feudatory tribal states mentioned with them were also presumably on the frontier'.[54]

The fourth category consisted of foreign potentates who symbolically recognized his sovereignty. These included Śrī Laṅkā and areas where the Kuṣāṇas and Śakas held sway. They sought to 'win the favour of the great emperor by personal attendance at his court, offering daughters in marriage, and asking permission for the use of imperial coins or soliciting imperial charters confirming them in the enjoyment of their territories'.[55]

Although the Allahabad pillar inscription enumerates this pattern of pan-Indian conquest as it were (with the exception of Mālwā), it does not state that Samudragupta performed the *Aśvamedha* sacrifice. However, a coin issued by him seems to commemorate it. The gold coin shows 'a horse standing before a sacrificial post (*yūpa*) on the obverse, and on the reverse the queen and the legend: Aśvamedha-parākramaḥ'.[56]

Some matters pertaining to the Allahabad pillar inscription do await clarification. Some scholars, following Keilhorn, take it as 'posthumous in nature'[57] but most scholars think otherwise as noted earlier. The fact that the *praśasti* does not mention the performance of the Aśvamedha supports this view. Scharfe points out that 'we notice that public rituals were frequent at the beginning of a dynasty: Puṣyamitra of the Śuṅga dynasty offered two horse sacrifices, Samudragupta of the Guptas four.'[58] What holds for the dynasty may not hold for the reign of an early member of the dynasty, although some have ventured to read evidence of Aśvamedha in the inscription.[59] The fact that the inscription does not mention the Vākāṭakas is more puzzling. As Hemchandra Raychaudhuri notes:

> It is not a little surprising that the Allahabad Praśasti contains no clear reference to the Vākāṭakas who are known to have dominated part of the region between Bundelkhand and the Pengaṅgā in the fifth century AD.[60]

Some explanations have been attempted but the fact nevertheless remains noteworthy.[61] The so-called Kācha coins and their relationship to Samudragupta and to the circumstances in which Samudragupta was selected to succeed remains obscure. The epithet *sarva-rājocchettā* is found on the coins, and coincides with Samudragupta's description in the inscription. Raychaudhuri is therefore disposed to identify the two. It is clear from the inscription Samudragupta was selected to succeed to the throne in a 'tense atmosphere'.[62]

> A special case was the appointment of Samudragupta as successor by his father

Candragupta I. As son of the heiress to the Licchavi kingdom, i.e., as the dauhitra of the Licchavi king, Samudragupta was entitled to succeed his maternal grandfather as soon as he came of age. Candragupta's second son would have claims to eventually succeed his father as king of the original Gupta kingdom. But 'under the glances of the withered face(s) of his relative(s) of equal birth ... [Samudragupta] was told by his father: "Rule the whole earth!"'[63]

It has been speculated that among the withered glances may have been those of 'Kācha ... the eldest brother of Samudragupta [who] headed the rebellion against him'.[64] This is far from certain. The selection of Samudragupta, however, is hinted at in another piece of epigraphic evidence, the Riddhapur inscription, in the epithet *tatpādaparigrhīta*.[65]

The martial achievements of Samudragupta imply a navy, although no direct reference to it is made in the inscription. 'Although there is no proof of this, we know that many islands in the Indian ocean were either conquered by the great Gupta monarch or submitted to him out of fear, thus clearly indicating his possession of a powerful navy'.[66]

John Keay even proposes that 'other islands' could mean 'the Indianised kingdoms of south-east Asia'.[67] Hemchandra Raychaudhuri suggests some indirect indication of a naval presence in the epigraph:

Some control over the islands in the neighbouring seas is possibly hinted at in the epithet *Dhanada-Varuṇendrāntakasama*, the equal of Dhanada (Kuvera, lord of wealth, guardian of the north), *Varuṇa* (the Indian Sea-god, the guardian of the west), Indra, king of the celestials and guardian of the east, and Antaka (Yama, god of death, and guardian of the south). The comparison of Samudragupta with these deities is apposite and probably refers not only to his conquests in all directions, but to his possession of immense riches, suzerainty over the seas, the spread of his fame to the celestial region and his extirpation of various kings. Inscriptions discovered in the Trans-Gangetic Peninsula and the Malay Archipelago testify to the activities of Indian navigators (e.g., the *Mahānāvika* from Raktamṛittikā mentioned in a Malayan epigraph) and military adventures in the Gupta Age.[68]

It is thus a major argument of this chapter that if one is looking for evidence to judge the presence or absence of historical sense among the Hindus, then the place to look for it are the epigraphic records left by the rulers. The very fact that such epigraphs are found in large numbers seems to quantitively testify to such a sense, and a critical examination of two famous inscriptions seems to confirm the same fact qualitatively. It only needs to be added that what was true of the north was also true of the south, as illustrated by the case of the Colas in medieval times. 'The exploits of both Rājarāja and his equally aggressive son'—covering a period from 985 AD to 1035 AD—'are celebrated in numerous inscriptions beginning from the eighth year of Rājarāja, whose earliest conquest was that of the Chera Kingdom.'[69]

II

The claim of the absence of a sense of history among the Hindus has sometimes being coupled with certain dimensions of Hindu culture in such a way as enhances the credibility of the claim. Some of these may border on the flippant, as when it might be claimed that just because in modern Hindi, the Indians use the same word for yesterday and tomorrow (*kal*) is proof enough that they possess no sense of the passage of time, to say nothing of history! But to take more serious aim, the following dimensions which have been identified as inimical to the presence of a sense of history among the Hindus: (1) belief in the eternality of the Vedas; (2) belief in the eternality of Sanskrit; (3) the presence of a cyclical notion of time; and (4) the caste system.

It is well known that in its eagerness to establish the eternality of the Vedas, the Mīmāṁsā School of Hindu philosophy went to great lengths to deny its historicity. Thus according to the Mīmāṁsā, 'no history and certainly no factual empirical knowledge can be had from the Veda; because in an eternal book, which is prior to all individual persons and things, there cannot be any preferences to persons or places.'[70] Even in relation to the events described in *smṛti*, as distinguished from *śruti*, literature, it is Kumārila's view that 'the numerous stories about creation and destruction, the rise and fall of nations, which are to be found in the *Purāṇas* and so on, are not factual; but they are only intended to teach some maxim such as that "the gross comes from the subtle", "earthly goods are impermanent", or "destiny is stronger than human effort".'[71]

Two points, however, need to be noted here. Although this happens to be the view of the Mīmāṁsā school within the Hindu tradition, it is not the only view regarding Vedic exegesis found in the tradition, an exegetical tradition which can be traced back to at least Yāska (fifth century BCE),[72] who refers to several contemporary schools of interpretation and 'cites the views of the Grammarians (*Vaiyākaraṇas*), the young and old ritualists (*yājñikas*), the Euhemerists (*aitihāsikas*) who took recourse to legendary lore for the explanation of Vedic stanzas, and the Ascetics (*parivrājakas*). The etymologists (*nairuktas*) are involved twenty times.'[73] Yāska was 'aware of other traditions of Vedic interpretation such as the Aitihāsikas (historical, for example, those who take Indra-Vṛtra battles as real incidents)',[74] which is significant because the Mahābhārata 'indicates that the Vṛtra legend ... can be understood symbolically'.[75] This tradition of multiple interpretations of the Vedas is a continuous one, as indicated by the *Ṛjvarthavyākhyā* of Durgāchārya who 'perhaps came after Skandasvāmī and Uvaṭa, but preceded Sāyaṇa',[76] and the commentary on it by Skandamaheśvara.[77] But a second point, with regard to the possession of historical sense by the Hindus, is more intriguing. It is sometimes held that a cyclical concept of time held by the Hindus goes against the grain so far as possessing a historical sense is concerned. This point is examined later on, but suffice it to mention here that the Mīmāṁsā school dispensed with this otherwise widespread concept of time in Hinduism in favour of a linear one, one supposedly more conducive for a sense of history.[78]

Belief in the eternality of any language, not just Sanskrit, is likely to compromise historical sense, because one is compelled under this view to conceal the phenomenon of historical (linguistic) change. The point has some force, but one must recognize that not everyone upheld such a view of language. For instance, Vācaspati Miśra did not 'believe in the eternity of words and sentences'[79] (although he might have in that of the letter).[80] Even more significant is the fact that the tradition distinguished between 'divine' and 'human' Sanskrit. As Michael Witzel writes:

Some have alleged, in more recent times, that the Indians indeed were not interested in, for example, the historical changes in their language(s). This again is a rather limited view, instigated by the Brahmanical interest in the unchangeability (*akṣara*) of Sanskrit. Sanskrit as the sacred language, the language of the gods, simply 'cannot' change. The gods speak the same Sanskrit, as we indeed should, nowadays, instead of Prakrit or Hindi. Pāṇini, when using *chandas*, thus refers to the sacred language, not to the *laukika Sanskrit of his area and time (bhāṣā)*. The beginnings of this attitude can be seen already in the authors of the Vedic texts. They have put such changes as they noticed into a social framework. The language of the gods has a socially higher status than that of men. Thus the gods used the higher, more correct form *rātrīm* 'the night' while men (and thus the author of the text) used *rātrim* (linguistically speaking, the gods' form is the older one). This attitude towards linguistic changes has been perpetuated in the dramas, where Brahmins and the king speak Sanskrit, but his wife and the servants various degrees of (the historically younger) colloquial Middle Indian Prakrtis.

On the other hand, the Vedic poets were keenly aware of past kings and dynasties and of their obligation of always creating new songs, praising gods and kings. They speak of a new *Yuga,* which would follow them, and in which they want to *preserve* their poetry (Ṛgveda 7.87.4) and which they indeed did until today, by the *chandas-ṛṣi-devatā* scheme latched on to the recitation of every hymn. They live *in a later Yuga* already (similar to the concept known from classical antiquity), and they expect another one to follow theirs.[81]

The cyclical notion of time in Hinduism has been seen more often than eternality of language as presenting an obstacle to the appearance of a historical sense among the Hindus, even when it is realized that 'time and the historical process are parts of a vast cyclical movement, but not, as in some cyclical versions of history, a simple cycle of birth, growth, death and then rebirth with a repetition of the past.'[82]

This view presents several difficulties. It has been pointed out that it is not the concept of time but of cosmology which is cyclical in Hindu thought,[83] and further that this concept itself appears in its full-fledged form only around the first century.[84] Nevertheless an account such as the following has come to be popularly associated with Hinduism:

By the time of the Upanishads Indian thinkers had had to face the antinomy of time, whose beginning and end are inconceivable, yet for which a lack of a beginning and an end is unacceptable. In the Artharva Veda hymns cited above, the answer was given in simple terms that Time is all-inclusive and rolls on endlessly, but in the passage quoted from the Maitri Upanishad, the antinomy was resolved by asserting that the Absolute, which is Brahman, is beyond Time, is in fact the Timeless, just as elsewhere the Absolute is beyond space and beyond the unending regressus of effect and cause. Time therefore remains, as the Rig Veda puts it, a wheel that revolves ceaselessly; it is measured by the sun, which passes above the recumbent earth, constantly pursuing its ordered round among the asterisms by which time is measured, in each annual revolution following the identical course which it followed in the preceding revolutions and, prophetically speaking, will follow in its revolutions to come.[85]

Michael Witzel repeats the argument,[86] but clarifies the issue when he writes:

Such a view of the time tempts one to ask the question: was it really important to record the events of the human past correctly or were they just variations on the constant theme of a repetitive Yuga cycle? Time was regarded as cyclical, a concept diametrically opposed to the linear concept of time we are used to in science. Telling sequential history was not limited to cultures with a sequential concept of time, such as the Hebrew one, but also found in others, such as that of Greece, where 'the father of history' Herodotus, in turn often recalls the example of Egyptian records. Such writings of sequential history are, of course, different from the Ṛgvedic concept of creating new songs, of incidental telling about former deeds of the gods, of earlier (*sādhyāḥ pūrve devāḥ*) and later gods (*devāḥ*), of ancient learned persons (*pūrve śrotriyā*, VadhBr.) or the semi-historical processes such as the colonization (Brahminization) of Eastern India (Videha) under Videgha Māthava and Gotama Rāhūgaṇa (Satapatha Brāhmaṇa).[87]

Michael Witzel then goes on to say that

After all these caveats we will see, in the sequel, that such a sequential view of history indeed also existed in India. Actually, both views, the sequential one and the cyclical one, are not mutually exclusive—if only a segment of the cycle is regarded or described. *Sub specie eternitatis*, of course, time was regarded as cyclical.[88]

Finally, the caste-bound character of Hindu society was also not perceived as conducive to the development of a sense of history. The anchoring of the system in the Puruṣa-Sūkta itself ahistoricised it according to P.V. Kane:

In the Puruṣasūkta (X.90.12) the brāhmaṇa, kṣatriya, vaiśya and śūdra are said to have sprung from the mouth, arms, thighs and feet of the supreme Puruṣa. In the very next verse the sun and the moon are said to have been born from the eye and mind of the Puruṣa. This shows that the composer of the hymn regarded the division of society into four classes to be very ancient and to be as natural and God-ordained as the sun and the moon.[89]

The static (or stable)[90] nature of the caste system would produce the same effect, even if it be admitted that the 'Indian class system was always somewhat fluid'.[91] Nor do the *varṇa*s fare well when taken severally. The *brāhmaṇas* were said to be too much into ritual to worry about history, and when they did feel so inclined they made things up to suit them. As Michael Witzel writes: 'furthermore we have to ask: how to treat the rest of evidence in Kalhaṇa, such as the stories about founding particular *agrahāras* as in the time of the mythical kings Kuśa and Lava. Such information was obviously based on local traditions of Brahmins who wanted to make their claims to certain stretches of land go back to the golden age of Rāma.'[92]

One would expect the *kṣatriyas* to have a firmer sense of history, but they too yield to the mythical temptation in their efforts to shore-up their pedigree. Michael Witzel notes that inventing pedigrees is not unique to India—the Achamaenids did it in Iran,[93] and even the Bible does it foı one 'can observe the extremes to which the New Testament had to go to show the descent of Jesus from King David, in spite of the fact that his father Joseph is reported, in some texts, not to have been his actual, somatic father'[94]—a piquancy which did not go unnoticed by Mahatma Gandhi.[95] This only goes to show that 'In all civilizations which stress the patrilinear descent such pedigrees are of great importance.'[96] In the Hindu case:

> In the Puranas these pedigrees (*vaṃśa*) have been systematized [so] as to trace back every local dynasty of the subcontinent to the mythical Sun (Sūryavaṃśa) or the Moon (Candravaṃśa) lineages. Even newcomers, such as the Huns, or the local dynasties of Nepal or Kashmir, simply 'must' go back to the beginning of mankind, or, at least to a well known ancient dynasty. This is what the Nepalese Licchavis (c. 300–750 AD) chose to do: they are traced, by their name, back to the contemporaries of the Buddha, the Licchavis of Vaiśāli, and they have simply invented the necessary link—interestingly not in their oldest surviving inscription of 464 AD, but in their chronicle and in their later, official lineage. In the late Middle Ages, the Later Malla, such as Pratāpa Malla of Kathmandu (in an inscription of NS 778 = 1657/8 AD), trace back their origin to the famous Karṇātaka king Nāndyadeva. He became a king of Nepal—only according to later tradition; he is not yet contained in the Gopālarāja-Vaṃśāvalī (written about NS 509 = 1388/9 AD).
>
> Newcomers can also resort to other tactics; they can claim descent from one or the other semi-divine nymph, a Nāginī—again nothing out of the way, as some of the earliest descendants of Manu, the first man, are reported to have had nymphs as their mothers (such as Purūravas' son Āyu). So did the Kārkoṭas of Kashmir who took over the country in c. 600 AD, and so did many local dynasties such as those of Bhadrāvakāśa, Chota Nagpur, Manipur, Bastar, and even the Śālivāhana king of Pratiṣṭhāna, the Pallavas, and especially also in the newly brahmanized countries of South-East Asia. The genealogies thus frequently serve for the limited purpose of political justification.[97]

The possession of a historical sense on the part of the Vaiśyas and the Śūdras would presumably be even harder to imagine.

Further examination of the point, however, produces a different outcome and the various *varṇas* seem to display a sense of history. In the case of Brāhmaṇas this need arises in the context of the *guruparamparā*; and in the case of Kṣatriyas in the context of dynastic history. This is to be expected. What is even more engaging if enigmatic is the sense for it displayed by the Vaiśyas. The famous Mandsor inscription of the guild of silk-weavers which belongs to the fifth century, 'shows us a guild of silk-weavers emigrating as a body from Lāṭa (the region of lower Narmadā) to Mandsor, and taking up many other crafts and possessions, from soldiering to astrology, but still maintaining its guild-consciousness'.[98] It was noted earlier how the Vaiśyas in the time of the Guptas (who were themselves Vaiśyas) took good care of the plates on which grants were inscribed. There was good commercial sense in doing so, but should historical be excluded? The oldest surviving documents from Nepal are 'land sale and mortgage documents dating back to 982/3 AD' which have 'remained in the possession of monasteries and in private ownership'.[99] In more recent times the Agrawalas have preserved an account of their origins with remarkable tenacity.[100]

Such evidence can probably be documented even in the case of the *śūdras*. There is even a Śūdraka era which dates from 170 BC.[101] But the explanation involved here has more to do with his being a king; even Manu testifies to the presence of *śūdra* kings (IV.61) and Kauṭilya to that of *śūdra* armies (IX.2). More to the point is the record of the preservation of their own account of the *varṇa* system by the *śūdras*. We owe this striking piece of evidence to Hyla Converse. She writes:

The account of the origin of caste that I am reporting was part of traditional lore recited in the early 1920's in classical Sanskrit poetry by a *śūdra bhāṭ* belonging to a śūdra enclave of a Hindu village near Khanewal and Mian Chanu in the Multan District of the Punjab. The area later became part of Pakistan, and there are no Hindus there now. The recitation was heard and partially noted down by Dr. Clyde B. Stuntz who was working in the area. I came to know of the account through a personal communication from Dr. Stuntz in 1963, when he heard of my interest in early Hinduism.

Dr. Stuntz had received a M.A. degree in Indo-Iranian Languages and Literature from Columbia University. He easily understood the *bhāṭ*'s Sanskrit and was able to identify it as early classical in form, indicating that this oral tradition was of ancient origin. The old *bhāṭ* who recited the story of how castes began, as well as other stories and genealogies of his *śūdra* group, was unable to read or write and did not understand Sanskrit as a language. But he had carefully and accurately memorized his precious accounts of the past, and he knew the general meaning of what he had memorized. He sadly complained that the younger people were no longer willing to undertake the arduous discipline of learning and transmitting their own oral traditions. He feared that when he died, all of his lore would be lost. A year or so later, when Dr. Stuntz returned to the village, hoping to spend more time with the old *bhāṭ* and take down his recitation more fully, the old man had died, and no one in the village had learned his lore.

Thus, all that remains of this ancient body of genealogies and stories of the mythic past is this one account which I am reporting. This *śūdra* account of the origin of castes differs entirely from Brahmanical ones, for it finds the source of *śūdra* servitude not in a primeval mythical ritual of creation, but in mythic history and an act of original injustice and betrayal.[102]

As for the story,

The story itself was simple and straightforward:

There was once a great and powerful man who ruled all over the land. He had four sons, all of whom were intelligent and gifted. When the man died he left his undivided property to all four sons. For a time they lived contentedly together, sharing the work and the wealth. Then the second son went off, with other warriors, to seek adventure and further riches. He asked his youngest brother to take care of his share of responsibilities for the property while he was gone and to see to whatever the family needed done, promising to reassume these burdens when he returned. The youngest brother generously agreed.

After a time the oldest brother decided to go to a hermitage and seek spiritual fulfillment. He too, asked his youngest brother to take over his chores and family cares. The third brother was very clever in business and became preoccupied in trading ventures and he also left his younger brother the everyday burdens of property and family.

So the youngest brother rendered service to the older three for some years. At last the older three brothers returned, each successful in his own endeavours. And they no longer wished to reassume the burdens, which their younger brother had carried for them in their absence. They preferred to continue to pursue their own interests unhampered. And so, instead of showing their youngest brother gratitude and honour for all he had done for them, the older three banded together and burdened him permanently with all those tasks that were distasteful to them, requiring him to be their servant. From then on, all the descendants of the younger brother were named Śūdras and were required to be the servants of the descendants of the three older brothers.[103]

It turns out then that far from the caste system proving subversive of historical sense in the Hindu context, each *varṇa* seems to exhibit a historical sense of its own.

A fifth problem associated with the acceptance of a historical sense on the part of the Hindus is their exaggerated sense of the past, which inclines one to say that they might possess a sense of antiquity but not history.[104] There is some substance to this charge as the Hindu scheme of *yugas* and *kalpas* involves mind-boggling figures. There is however, enough evidence now to indicate that both outsiders and insiders to the Hindu tradition are aware of this distinction, and moreover that rational explanation of at least part of tendency towards chronological exaggeration may be available. The first major foreign source for Hindu chronology is Megathenes.[105] The restrained nature of the figures led the translator to remark: 'it is not known from what sources Megathenes derived these figures, which are extremely modest when compared with those of Indian chronology, where, as in geology, years are hardly reckoned in years but in myriads.'[106] More than a thousand years later Al-Bīrūnī remarks that 'the Hindus do not consider it wearisome to reckon with huge numbers, but rather enjoy it',[107] but nevertheless proceeds to point out that those eras they use which 'vie with each other in antiquity'[108] are such 'as not only astronomers, but also other people, think it wearisome and unpractical to use them'.[109] He notes that in their place they employ other eras, what we might call eras of history, as associated with Śrī Harṣa, Vikramāditya, Śaka, Valabha, and Gupta.[110] Even more to the point is Michael Witzel's explanation of how errors tend to creep into the use of eras because of a cultural commitment, as it were, to reach back to the beginning of the Kali Yuga, and that 'the concept of Kali Yuga, as the period we live in, plays a great role that has not been appreciated in the evaluation of chronicles such as *vaṃsāvalīs*'.[111] The point to note is that the slippage from history to antiquity is not a mere flight of fancy, but the consequence (or cause) of systemic errors, such as counting contemporary dynasties as successive, etc.[112]

It was noted earlier that the ancient Indian inscriptions tend to be dated in the regnal year of the kings, or often in an era that is not specified. This was the case with the two inscriptions—those of Rudradāman and Samudragupta—discussed earlier and seems to encourage the belief that the Hindus lacked a sense of history and chronology. A. L. Basham writes:

> Until the 1st century BC there is no good evidence that India had any regular system of recording the year of an advent by dating in a definite era like the A.U.C. of Rome or the Christian era of medieval and modern Europe. Early inscriptions are dated if at all in the regnal year of the ruling king. The idea of dating over a long period of time from a fixed year was almost certainly introduced into India by the invaders of the Northwest, who have left the earliest inscriptions thus dated in India. Unfortunately the Indians did not adopt a uniform era, and a number of systems of dating were in use from that time onwards, the chief of which, in order of importance, are as follows.[113]

This passage creates the further impression that reckoning from a fixed point was introduced in India by foreigners. All this, however, must be viewed in the light of another set of facts. For instance, 'the traditional date of Mahāvīra's death is fixed near the end of the rainy season in 527 BC; it is from this date that Jainas count the Vīranirvāṇa period, *the longest continuous "era" in Indian history*.'[114] Thus it is simply not true that Indians had no reckoning from a fixed era. The remark holds true only of the epigraphic evidence so far available and should not be transferred uncritically to the Hindu or Indic mentality. Another point in relation to this era deserves mention. 'One Jaina source (Hemacandra's *Pariśiṣṭaparva*: viii, 341) places this event in 427 BC.'[115] If this amendment is accepted then the chronology calculated on this basis purely from Indian sources almost coincides with the current chronology of ancient India evolved by Western scholarship over the past two hundred years.[116] The Parinirvāṇa of the Buddha, could also provide another such fixed point, although in this case, as in the case of the Vīranirvāṇa, there is even greater debate as to the exact point.[117] But even when there is a difference as to where the point is to be fixed exactly, it does not compromise the claim that calculation from a fixed point was in use, with the attendant sense of history involved. What is true is that evidence of this kind from *Hindu* sources is not available. As further evidence of the existence of historical sense in general, one may add that 'according to the unanimous tradition of the Buddhists, the Buddha died in the 8th year of the reign of Ajātaśatru'.[118]

In any case, the very fact that Hindu or ancient Indian kings employ a number of eras also testifies to their sense of history, although this fact complicates our chronological computations.[119] The example of the Harṣa era should suffice. Dr Devahuti lists two inscriptions of Harṣa and seven others as generally believed to be dated in the Harṣa era of 606 AD.[120] Al-Bīrūnī has an interesting note about this era. He writes:

> ... His [i.e. Sri-Harsha's] era is used in Mathura and the country of Kanoj. Between Sri Harsha and Vikramaditya there is an interval of 400 years, as I have been told by the inhabitants of that region. However, in the Kashmirian calendar I have read that Sri Harsha was 664 years later than Vikramaditya. In face of this discrepancy I am in perfect uncertainty....[121]

Dr Devahuti suggests the following resolution of this difficulty.

> To demonstrate the application of the various eras to a given date, the year 400 of Yazdajird, Al-Bīrūnī calculates the commencement of the Harsha era according to the Mathura and Kanauj tradition, which placed Harsha 400 years before Vikramāditya, i.e. in 457 BC. But on the authority of the Kashmir calendar, Harsha being '664 years later than Vikramāditya', the Harsha era should be placed in AD 606–7. We think it was this era, which was prevalent in Al-Bīrūnī's time in Mathurā and Kanauj. It seems that the inhabitants of the region deliberately misguided the Muslim scholar in order to impress him with the antiquity of the era they used. Al-Bīrūnī, though in possession of the correct information through the Kashmir source, naturally placed greater reliance on local tradition, which seemed more authentic on its face value. It is well known that he misunderstood, similarly, the traditions relating to the Gupta era. His critical pen, however, has preserved for us the valuable information he got from the Kashmir Calendar, that Sri Harsha was '664 years later than Vikramāditya'.[122]

She then proceeds to add:

> The astronomical data provided by the *Harsha-charita* helps us to determine the date of Harsha's birth in AD 590. All the circumstances of that period support the view that Harsha ascended the throne at an early age after his elder brother was killed in his early youth. The Harsha era, beginning in AD 606, when Harsha would be only 16, is in accordance with this fact.[123]

It also resolves a slight discrepancy introduced by Xuanzang's account.[124]

Al-Bīrūnī himself enumerates no less than eleven eras and distinguishes between a set of six eras which 'vie in antiquity' and another set of five[125] in favour of the former ones which had been abandoned. This itself implies a distinction between antiquity and history. It is therefore mildly surprising that he castigates the Hindus for lacking a sense of chronology on the one hand and on the other enumerates the many eras they employ. The same sense of history is indicated by the fact that according to Al-Bīrūnī, Hindus celebrate a historic victory as a festival. Although he is somewhat sceptical about the facts, his account runs as follows:

> The 2nd of the month Caitra is a festival to the people of Kashmir, called Agdus (?), and celebrated on account of a victory gained by their king, Muttai, over the Turks. According to their account he ruled over the whole world. But this is exactly what they say of most of their kings. However, they are incautious enough to assign him to a time not much anterior to our time, which leads to their lie being found out. It is, of course, not impossible that a Hindu should rule (over a huge empire), as Greeks, Romans, Babylonians, and Persians have done, but all the times not much anterior to our own are well known. (If, therefore, such had been the case, we should know it.) Perhaps the here mentioned king ruled over the whole of India, and they know of no other country but India and of no other nations but themselves.[126]

There is however some evidence which actually supports this fact, if Muttai is read as a reference to King Muktāpīḍa of the Kārkoṭa Dynasty of Kashmir, who is said to have defeated the Turks in the eighth century thrice.[127]

III

We may now revert to the discussion of the point that different cultures may have different ways of expressing their sense of history, and this may also be reflected in their choice of the medium for doing so. Stones and not parchment seems to have the medium of choice in ancient India. Even in the case of documents[128] the sense of history finds its niche in slightly unusual places, such as the colophons of manuscripts. The question of manuscripts, however, raises an important issue of their survival, a problem less acute in the case of inscriptions. It might be possible, with only slight exaggeration, to maintain the thesis that historical records in the broadest sense may have abounded but have simply perished for climatic reasons, combined with political factors. Michael Witzel writes:

> A little used source of history have been the colophons of manuscripts which often mention the name of the reigning monarch and other historically interesting details. This is due to the fact that in India proper most mss. are only of relative late date. Except for the desert areas of Gujarat/Rajasthan, mss. have not survived much more than 500 years, and Hindus in general did not care much for their preservation as only the living, recited word, in the mouth of the teacher, poet or priest was important. Fortunately, the Jainas and Buddhists preserved their texts as far as the early ninth century AD (in dated form), and a few older undated ones, so much so that when Bendall first made use of their colophons for historical purposes at the Berlin congress about a hundred years ago, he was simply not believed at first. In Nepal the temperate climate and the almost complete absence of Muslim incursions worked together to preserve these old mss. Such ms. colophons, which also contain much of other valuable and so far unused information, such as on local personal and geographical names, religious trends, etc., should be used for the elucidation of 'dark spots' in the history of particular local areas and their political history, say, for parts of Orissa, Kerala, and Gujarat.[129]

This is significant as indicative of the kind of evidence of a sense of history now lost to us. There is evidence that detailed administrative records were kept in Mauryan times. The office of the *akṣapaṭala* as detailed in the Arthaśāstra (2.7.1) provides such convincing evidence of this[130] that Hartmut Scharfe is led to remark:

> In view of the careful bookkeeping in the *akṣa-paṭala* the virtual absence of archives and chronicles in India is surprising; but the climate would destroy most documents. The frequent change of administrative centres as a result of the rise of new dynasties with a strictly regional power base further prevented the development of an archival tradition.[131]

There is, however, enough evidence of the presence of such a tradition.[132] It is even mentioned in the *Manusmṛti* (X.55; IX.332; VIII.255) which is usually placed between the Mauryan and the Gupta Period.[133] The Allahabad Pillar inscription depicts suppliant kings seeking confirmation through royal decrees.[134] Once again no trace of them is left. Zuanzang clearly refers to records[135] kept at the provincial level, which also are no longer available.[136]

An extreme case of the conspiracy of the negative forces in relation to the manuscript tradition is provided by Kashmir, where 'no mss. older than c. 1500 AD remain. Local Hindu and Muslim chroniclers agree in blaming the Sultans Sikander and Ali (1389-1419/20) for their wholesale destruction by burning and dumping them in the Dal Lake.'[137]

For further evidence of 'historical' writing one turns to: (1) the so called *thyasaphu*, usually known only to Nepalese specialists. These private chronicles were kept by Nepalese priests and other high caste men. They are called *thyasphu*, '"folded books", as they are written on leporello-form cardboard type books. They are invariably written in medieval or more modern Newari and are very detailed',[138] (2) a 'very rare biography written by a 17th-century Jain businessman, Banarasidas, hailing from Jaumpur but living in Agra', the *Ardhakathānak*,[139] and (3) temple histories such as the Madala Panji of Orissa, and the collection of inscriptions at the Tirupati temple.[140]

One could now turn one's attention to such literary evidence which might have a bearing on the historical sense of the Hindus as has survived. This would include the Vedas, the Purāṇas, the tradition of historical *kāvyas* in Sanskrit, and literature in general.

The problem with the evidence provided by the Vedas is that it has been constantly reworked. 'How this reworking took place can be closely studied if we compare the Ṛg Vedic form of such a popular tale as that of Purūravas and Urvaśī (RV 10.95), with its form in Śatapatha Brāhmaṇa 11.5.1 or the Baudhāyana Śrauta Sūtra 18.44, in the Mahābhārata I.70, and in Kālidāsa's Kāvya.'[141] So what we have here are materials for the cultural history of Hinduism rather than history itself. This has the unfortunate consequence that the 'ancient historical tradition of India, as found in the Mahābhārata and the Purāṇas, thus is flawed from the beginning: it is not history but the bardic reworking of the old epic tradition, often based on Vedic tradition itself'.[142] However, while not history itself, it has provided enough material for the writing of one, at least at the hands of H. C. Raychaudhuri.[143]

What is significant in it, however, is the 'idea of genealogy', which in this particular case may be beyond recovery, but which provided the model for the writing up of genealogies in later, more historical times. That these royal genealogies can be of historical value has been demonstrated painstakingly by Michael Witzel's work on the *Gopālarājavaṁśāvalī* of Nepal. It was discovered a hundred years ago by Bendall and initially even aroused some scepticism.

Its text consists of two parts. The first part, which is in Sanskrit, presents a legendary account of early kings, followed by a detailed account of King Śivadeva (Nepal Saṁvat 219=1098 AD), and towards the end records a description of an Islamic incursion into the valley under Sams ud-Din in November 1349[144] and the victory of king Jayasthiti Malla c.1389 AD, after which it trails off. The second part covers the period from Nepal Samvat 177 (=1057 AD)—the year of birth of king Śivadeva—to Nepal Saṁvat 508 (=1388 AD), that is, until a few years before the death of king Jayasthiti Malla. It is also initially in Sanskrit but with occasional entries in old Newari; the account from 1219 AD being entirely in old Newari.[145] The significance of such works becomes apparent when one realizes that 'the core of historical tradition in India was the genealogical records. These have remained constant in the Indian scene throughout the centuries and in fact up to the present day.'[146] It should therefore not come as a surprise that the *Gopālarājavaṁśāvalī* is 'certainly not the only text of its sort. There are more ... perhaps many more than we might expect. The *Vaṁśāvalīs* from Himachal Pradesh are comparatively well known due to Atkinson's work. Other *Vaṁśāvalīs* are the Katyuris of Kangra, the Chands of Kumaon (c. 1150 AD) and the Panwars of Garwal. In Rajasthan, there are a large number of *Vaṁśāvalīs* dealing both with the royal houses as well as some high caste persons. In this region they are maintained by special classes of people.'[147] As is well known, in 'the Purāṇas the genealogies are carefully preserved and follow an historical order'[148] and F. E. Pargiter[149] famously tried to reconstruct the history of pre-Buddhist India from these. What is interesting here is that while the 'stress on local dynastic history and the size of the area involved'[150] may 'have prevented the "composition of a universal" history of South Asia ... even this is not altogether absent. It has been attempted in the Purāṇas, interestingly again in the Brahmanical guise of dynastic history, through the linking of all royal families of the subcontinent with their mythical ancestors, Manu and his sons.'[151]

The Purāṇas are one manifestation of the *itihāsa-purāṇa* tradition of Indic civilization.

> The *itihāsa-purāṇa* tradition has three main constituents—myth, genealogy, and historical narrative. The remote past was described in the form of myths and probably fabricated genealogies. There is so far no means of checking the authenticity of these genealogies. The more immediate past was recorded almost entirely in the form of genealogies filled out with historical narrative. Some of these genealogies can be checked with other sources to establish their historical authenticity. The

historical literature of the post-Gupta period is almost exclusively historical narrative, but the authors of this literature show a familiarity with the *itihāsa-purāṇa* tradition which is frequently used as a the source for references to myths and genealogies. Inscriptions of the post-Gupta period referring to the antecedents of local kings also make the connection with the *itihāsa-purāṇa* tradition.[152]

The historical narratives constitute a class of classical Sanskrit literature. To this class belong such works as: (1) The *Navasāhasāṅkacarita* of Parimala Padmagupta (c.1005); (2) The *Vikramaṅkadevacarita* of Bilhaṇa (11th century); (3) The *Rājataraṅgiṇī* of Kalhaṇa (c.1148–9); (4) The *Pṛthvīrājavijaya* of Jayānaka (c.1192); (5) The *Dvyāśrayamahākāvya* of Hemacandra Sūri (12th century); (6) The *Rāmacarita* of Sandhyākara (12th century); (7) The *Kīrtikaumudī* of Someśvaradeva (13th century); (8) The *Sukṛtasaṁkīrtana* of Arisiṁha (c.1229); (9) The *Vasantavilāsa* of Bālacandra Sūri (c.1300); (10) The *Hammīramahākāvya* of Nayacandra Sūri (15th century); (11) The *Madhurāvijaya* of Gaṅgādevī (c.1371); and (12) The *Saluvābhyudaya* of Rājanātha Diṇḍima (c.1480).[153]

To these one must add the famous prose romance of Bāṇa, the *Harṣacarita*, which belongs to the seventh century and the *Gauḍavaho* of Vākpatirāja in Prakrit which belongs to the eighth century. These works suffer from certain limitations such as the use of poetic conceit and their obviously panegyrical character but they do serve to draw attention to the fact that 'there are more historical texts than the legendary Purāṇas,'[154] and that these 'have been very little used so far'[155] as source material for sober history. Their significance is obvious when one considers the fact that *Rāmacarita* of Sandhyākara 'can be read as applying either to the legendary Rāma of Ayodhyā or to the historical king Rāmapāla of Bengal, who was the poet's contemporary and patron'.[156] That such a work should be written under the aegis of the Buddhist Pāla dynasty offers comment on the state of Hindu-Buddhist relations in medieval India. The fact that the court ladies of the Vijayanagara Empire wrote such historical epics, as documented by Julie Hiebert, has important cultural implications.[157] Sanskrit literature in general also provides some evidence of a sense of history. For instance, various fields within it, such as grammar, have their own accounts of the past. Pāṇini (c. fourth century BCE) refers to sixty-four previous grammarians[158] and the etymologist Yāska (c. fifth century BC) refers to grammatical, ritualist, euhemerist, and ascetic approaches to Vedic exegesis.[159] The texts on *Āyurveda*, similarly refer to early figures, the *Carakasaṁhitā* (I.7.14) mentioning over fifty. Although Bharata's *Nāṭyaśāstra* (I.26-39) (anachronistically) lists a hundred experts in dramaturgy and the *Arthaśāstra* texts (for example, Kauṭilya I.15) refer to previous savants in the field. Even the *ṚgVeda* (VII.87.4) speaks of earlier and later *yugas* and Vedic recitation preserves lost tonal accents in early Sanskrit.[160] The manner in which Patañjali has been assigned to the second century BC is also instructive.[161] As Fritz Staal points out, 'the argument is of special interest because it illustrates how the Sanskrit grammarians' carefully recorded observations on the use of tenses could also be used for the determination of data.'[162] Dramas are also instructive in this respect. Those with historical themes such as the Malavikāgnimitra, Mudrārākṣasa, and Devīcandragupta display a sense of history, while a number of medieval dramas from Nepal provide considerable historical information.[163] But beyond this, it has even been claimed that the Sanskrit poets themselves may have possessed a sense of history. Some have read a covert allusion to the 'link of kings beginning (?) with the Samudragupta' in *āsamudrakṣitīśanām* (*Raghuvaṁśa* I.5); to the Gupta kings in *goptre guptamendriyaḥ* (I.55) and *anvāsya goptā gṛhiṇī-sahāyaḥ* (II.24); and to Kumāragupta in *ikṣucchāyaniṣādinyas tasya goptur guṇodyam*; *ākumārakathodghātam śāligopyo jagur yaśaḥ* (III.2).[164]

H. C. Raychaudhuri does not go so far but he does remark:

The capture and liberation of the southern kings [by Samudragupta] notably the ruler of Koṭṭūra near Mt. Mahendragiri remind us of the following lines of Kālidāsa's *Raghuvaṁśam*:

Gṛihīta-pratimuktasya sa dharma-vijayī nṛipah
Śriyaṁ Mahendra-nāthasya jahāra natu medinīm

'The righteous conqueror (Raghu) took away from the lord of the Mahendra Mountain, who was made captive and then released, his glory but not his territory.'[165]

IV

Another piece of evidence, which might dispose one to a reconsideration of the proposition that Hindus lacked a sense of history, pertains to the medieval period. It is contained in the following excerpted conversation between Steven J. Gelberg, a member of the Hare Krishna movement and Shrivatsa Goswami of Vṛndāvana on the Bhakti movement.

SJG: Shrivatsa, could you now describe the development of the bhakti movement–or conglomeration of *bhakti* movements–from roughly the eleventh to the eighteenth centuries? Who were the major figures and what were the important movements during this devotional renaissance?

SG: To begin with, let me cite a very interesting literary document, dated in the fifteenth century, called the Bhāgavata Māhātmya or 'the Glories of the Bhāgavatam'. In it, there's discourse between the sage Nārada and personified Bhakti, appearing in the form of a young woman, says, 'Oh sage, I was born in the Draviḍa land and grew up to maturity in Karṇāṭaka. At some places in Mahārāṣṭra I was respected, but after coming to Gujarat I became old and decrepit ... . I was subjected to live in that stage for a long time and I became weak and sluggish ... . But after reaching Vṛndāvana I became rejuvenated, and endowed with enviable beauty. Thus, I appear quite young with a lovely form.' Later, in response, Nārada says to Bhakti, 'Vṛndāvana really deserves praise, as it is due to its contact that *bhakti* was rejuvenated as a young woman and where she now gleefully dances.'

So this gives, beautifully, the historical development of medieval *bhakti* tradition. The *bhakti* movement took birth in South India with the Dravidian saints, the Alvars, and so on. Then a little later, Rāmānuja, the first systematic philosopher of *bhakti*, appeared in Tamil country. He was the first major ācārya to declare *bhakti,* aside from *jñāna*, as a legitimate path to realize God. After Rāmānuja, the next devotional thinker was Madhva, who was born in Karṇāṭaka at the end of the twelfth century. After that, the movement got a big boost from different saints who appeared throughout India, including Mahārāṣṭra, during the fourteenth, fifteenth, and sixteenth centuries. These centuries were very crucial for the growth of the *bhakti* movement. But the *bhakti* movement did not attain its highest development, as the passage implies, until it reached Vṛndāvana, of course, in the form of Caitanya Mahāprabhu because it was Caitanya who, along with His followers the six Gosvāmīs, was the founder of Vṛndāvana in the early part of the sixteenth century. So, the whole history of *bhakti* movement is summarized here quite beautifully.

SJG: When is the latest the Bhāgavata Māhātmya could have been written?

SG: According to modern secular scholars, it cannot be any later than a fifteenth-century work.

SJG: How is it that a fifteenth-century text is describing Vṛndāvana, which was not established as an active pilgrimage centre until the sixteenth century? Vṛndāvana was already known, of course, as a sacred place of Krishṇa's historical descent, but it was nothing more than a remote forest until Caitanya Mahāprabhu and the Gosvāmīs went there and developed it an active spiritual centre in the early sixteenth century. Before that, certainly, no *bhakti* movement flourished there. How do you explain that?

SG: There was my intriguing question to Professor A. L. Basham. He visited the Philosophy Department at Benares Hindu University some years ago and gave a talk on 'The Hindu Sense of Time and History'. He claimed that except for one or two minor works, Hindus have no historical documents, and they have no sense of time and history. So I quoted these lines from Bhāgavata Māhātmya, which scholars agree is no later than fifteenth century, and asserted that this description provides a very accurate historical picture of the *bhakti* movement and its development. I said, 'How do you explain this? How can you say that the Hindus have no sense of past? I will say that they have even a sense of future! Vyāsa has described, in vivid details, *bhakti*, its historical growth, and its establishment in Vṛndāvana.'[166]

V

Evidence in support of this new perspective is next encountered in the work of Heinrich von Stietencron—and in a very new form—not in written word but in plastic art. Stietencron began with the same 'trite observation'[167] (his own words), that 'to the modern viewer, therefore, there appears to be an ahistoric and non-political attitude in indigenous Indian art which, true to the alleged spiritual quest for the ultimate unchanging reality, did not bother to preserve in stone the transitory achievements of mortal kings'.[168] Like Professor Witzel, he eventually arrived at a very different conclusion: that even in artistic representations the Hindus displayed a sense of history. Consider, for instance, the depiction of Śiva as Gaṅgādhara.

> The myth tells the story of the descent of the celestial river Gaṅgā to the earth in order to make her purifying waters available to mankind, particularly for the purification rituals after death. A mortal, Bhāgīratha, after practising austerities for a long time, obtains Gaṅgā's consent to come down to earth. But in order to save the earth from the danger of bursting under the impact of the cascade of heavenly waters, Lord Śiva is requested to receive the celestial river on his mighty head.
>
> Śiva agrees and thus becomes mediator between heaven and earth in one of the important cosmogonic acts, which brings life-giving and sanctifying waters to the human world. It is for this act that he is praised as Gaṅgādhara, the god 'who carries Gaṅgā.'
>
> Gaṅgā has doubts whether Śiva will be strong enough to withstand the impact of her fall. Convinced of her own strength she believes that the power of her descent will push Śiva down into the nether worlds. But Śiva, stretching out one or two locks of his hair like a hammock, receives her with perfect ease and immediately punishes her for her self-conceit; for many years she roams about in the endless labyrinth of his crown of matted hair without finding her way out. And it is only on account of the renewed and powerful austerities of Bhāgīratha that Śiva finally releases the thoroughly humiliated goddess.[169]

So far we are in the realm of myth. To enter in the realm of history we need to recall that medieval Indian history in the south was characterized by rivalry between the Cālukya dynasty of Bādāmi and the Pallava dynasty of Tiruchirāpalli in the seventh century.[170] Stietencron draws out attention to the fact that

> The first image of Gaṅgādhara based on this form of myth was created at Tiruchirāpalli

in the Pallava country during the reign of king Mahendravarman I (ca. 610–30). This king was in bitter conflict with his neighbour, king Durvinīta of the Western Gaṅgā dynasty, who had broken away from the century-old feudal alliance with the Pallavas and joined the camp of their rivals, the Cālukyas of Bādāmi. Durvinīta attacked the young king Mahendravarman from the North-West, and simultaneously, the Cālukya armies invaded Mahendravarman's North-Eastern territories in Veṅgī. The Pallava kingdom seemed truly in great danger until Mahendravarman achieved a victory over his 'foremost enemies' at Pullalūr, ca. 15 miles North of his capital Kāñcī. It is to be added that the Gaṅgā kings were Jains while Mahendravarman, formerly also a Jain, had become a devotee of Śiva.

It was after this victory that the first Gaṅgādhara image of the type described above was created in south India. It shows the four-armed Śiva, hailed by celestials, standing in leisurely pose with one leg supported by his bull Nandin, as he gracefully stretches out a lock of hair to receive the descending goddess Gaṅgā who appears comparatively small and insignificant. To any contemporary the message of this image was clear enough. Just as Śiva stood in ease against the impact of (the water of the river) Gaṅgā who, in her self-conceit, had believed she could send him to hell, even so the Śaiva king Mahendravarman stood in each against the impact of (the army of) the Gaṅgās who, in their self-conceit, had believed they could destroy the Pallava king. No image of any other form of Śiva and no other myth could have served to translate this actual historical situation more effectively into a work of religious art.

We can be sure the artists and kings and the educated public were conscious of this message of the Gaṅgādhara image because it retained it direct allusion to the Gaṅgā dynasty during the following centuries ... .[171]

A more dramatic example of the interaction between the political history and the history of art is provided by the famous depiction of Viṣṇu's incarnation as the Boar (*varāhāvatāra*) in the Udayagiri cave. Three interpretations of this depiction are presented below. The reader may wish to note that they become progressively more historical, in accordance with the assumption of the degree of the sense of history on the part of the Hindus entertained by each scholar.

The first interpretation is that by A. L. Basham. He writes:

Perhaps the most immediately impressive of all Guptan sculptures is the Great Boar, carved in relief at the entrance of a cave at Udayagiri near Bhīlsā. The body of the god Viṣṇu, who became a mighty boar to rescue the earth from the cosmic ocean, conveys the impression of a great primeval power working for good against the forces of chaos and destruction, and bears a message of hope, strength and assurance. The greatness of the god in comparison with his creation is brought out by the tiny female figure of the personified earth, clinging to his tusk. The deep feeling, which inspired the carving in this figure, makes it perhaps the only theriomorphic image in the world's art, which conveys a truly religious message to modern man.[172]

There is virtually no historical element in Basham's artistic appreciation of this piece. This emerges in the interpretation by H. C. Raychaudhuri who writes:

According to sacred legends Viṣṇu in the shape of a Boar had rescued the earth in the aeon of universal destruction. It is significant that the worship of the Boar Incarnation became widely popular in the Gupta-Chalukya period. The poet Viśākhadatta actually identifies the *man* in whose arms the earth found refuge when harassed by the *Mlechchhas*, who 'shook the yoke of servitude from the neck' of his country, with the *Varāhītanu* (Boar form) of the Self-Existent Being. Powerful emperors both in the north and south recalled the feats of the Great Boar, and the mightiest ruler of a dynasty that kept the Arabs at bay for centuries actually took the title of *Ādivarāha* or the Primeval Boar. The Boar Incarnation then symbolized the successful struggle of Indians against the devastating floods issuing from the regions outside their borders that threatened to overwhelm their country and civilization in a common ruin.[173]

The reference to the poet Viśākhadatta in the passage just cited is an allusion to:

the concluding verse of Viśākhadatta's drama Mudrārākṣasa which, while dealing with events to the time of Candragupta Maurya, refers indirectly also to Candragupta II, who was the poet's contemporary and may have been his patron. In Jan van Buitenen's translation this verse reads:

The Self-Begotted God did once assume
The fitting body of a mighty Boar
And on his snout did save the troubled Earth,
Nurse of all beings, when she was deluged:
Now, terrified by the barbarians hordes,
She has sought shelter in our king's strong arms:
May Candragupta, our most gracious king,
Whose people prosper and whose kinsmen thrive,
For long continue to protect the land![174]

Heinrich von Stietencron goes on to say:

Whether the Udayagiri image is an illustration of the poet's words, or whether the poet was in turn inspired by the image, cannot be determined with certainty, nor is it relevant in the present context. That such identification of kings and gods was not simply flattering talk of eager panegyrists, but formed part of a royal ideology of divine kingship and was proclaimed by kings in their own inscriptions is shown, among many other instances, by the Allahabad pillar inscription of Candragupta's father Samudragupta.[175]

Stietencron is more willing than either Basham or Raychaudhuri to concede a sense of history to the Hindus, and espies an even more specific historical significance in the sculpture depiction under discussion. He writes:

There is a special feature in the Varāha relief of Udayagiri which is repeated nowhere else. The ocean out of which the dominating image of Varāha rises with great strength is represented with meticulous care by its endless waves, and again twice in personified form as man standing in this ocean with a water-pot in his hands. The two river goddesses Gaṅgā and Yamunā are seen flowing towards him.

Later images do not show the ocean at all. But here the ocean (Sanskrit: *samudra*) has a special meaning. A word play takes on plastic form. Just as Varāha issuing from the mighty (ocean) *samudra* rescued the earth from *asura* oppression, even so did Candragupta II, issuing from his mighty (father) *Samudragupta* rescue the earth from *asura* (i.e. Western Kṣatrapa) oppression. The person with the water-pot standing in the ocean has thus a double meaning. He is the ocean in anthropomorphic form, but he is also an image of Candragupta's father Samudragupta.

The ocean was dropped altogether in later representations, since it could not carry similar connotations with other donors.[176]

VI

Thus far from lacking a sense of history the Hindus even imparted a plastic dimension to historiography. If this is so then this provides added force to the argument developed by Professor Witzel that Hindu historiography suffered serious obscuration during the period of Islamic occupation, as this period also involved the destruction of holy images and temples which were one form of material in which such history was preserved. The numerous internal dynastic evolutions would prove equally destructive.

It should also be remembered that Hindu learning and the Hindu educational system possessed a marked oral character, a feature also noticed by Megasthenes.[177] In fact, this has been identified by Professor Kane as one of its weaknesses,[178] a weakness which made it particularly vulnerable to historical vicissitudes resulting from foreign conquests. Al-Bīrūnī's statement that as a result of Mahmūd's devastating raids 'Hindu sciences have retired far away from those parts of the country conquered by us, and have fled to places where our hand cannot yet reach, to Kashmir, Benares, and other places'[179] becomes far more significant than it would be in the light of this *embodied* character of Hindu learning.

The claim that the sheer destruction caused by political vicissitudes is responsible for the mistaken impression that the ancient Indians kept no historical records (because they are lost) however begs credulity. It sounds too superficial and smooth a response to the charge that ancient Indians possessed no sense of history, to the point of sounding apologetic. Our task then is to render it more plausible. One may begin by starting with an extreme position stated as follows: the perfect genocide is one, which never occurred, because no one was left behind to tell the story. The point to be made is that the scale of destruction can be such as destroys the very evidence of that destruction. One then faces what might be called an evidentiary 'black hole'. Some evidence on the nature and scope of such destruction involved in the foreign invasions to which *ancient* India was subjected, needs to be introduced at this stage.

After the fall of the Mauryan and then the Śuṅga Empire, north India experienced a major political upheaval in the form of numerous invasions.

> The period of 500 years between 200 BC and 300 AD was a very dark and dismal one for Northern India. The fertile plains of the Punjab and the Gangetic valley were subjected during this period to one foreign invasion after another. First came the Greeks, who under Demetrius and Menander (c. 190–150 BC) were able to penetrate right up to Patna in Bihar, and then came Scythians and the Parthians (c. 100 BC to 50 AD). These ... were followed by the Kushanas, who succeeded in overrunning practically the whole of northern India by the middle of the 2nd century AD.[180]

The *Gārgīsaṁhitā* section of the *Yugapurāṇa* assesses the damage caused by the invasion of Śakas as follows: *caturbhāgaṁ tu śastreṇa nāśayiṣyanti prāṇinām. Śakāḥ śeṣaṁ hariṣyanti caturbhāgaṁ svakaṁ puraṁ. Vinaṣṭe śakarājye tu śūnyā pṛthvī bhaviṣyati*. In other words these wars of conquest reduced the population of North India by 'one half, 25 per cent being killed and 25 percent being enslaved and carried away'.[181] The Yuga Purāṇa (167) further informs us that during this period even women took to ploughing, presumably as a result of this decimation.[182] Indian opinion at the time seemed to blame Aśoka's pacifism for this disaster, for the same Gārgīsaṁhitā declares: 'the fool established the so-called conquest of dharma' (*sthāpayisyati mohātmā vijayaṁ nāma dhārmikam*).[183] This is not the place, however, to assess Aśoka's rule but in this context it is necessary to point out that some Indologists seem to overlook the implication of the scale of the destruction involved. While describing the state administration under the Mauryas, Hartmut Scharfe writes (as noted earlier): 'In view of the careful bookkeeping in the *akṣa-paṭala* the virtual absence of archives and chronicles in India is surprising; but the climate would destroy most documents.'[184] Without discounting the role of climate one might wish to urge that the reason may not be just climatic but also 'climactic', if we use that expression to refer to the cataclysmic invasions just alluded to. Professor A. L. Basham perhaps comes closer to assessing the significance of these invasions when he connects them with the Hindu conceptualizations of the Kaliyuga. He writes:

> The end of the Kali-yuga, according to many epic passages, is marked by confusion of classes, the overthrow of established standards, the cessation of all religious rites, and the rule of cruel and alien kings. Soon after this the world is destroyed by flood and fire. This view is propounded strongly in texts, which date from about the beginning of the Christian era, when alien kings did in fact rule much of India, and established practices were shaken by heresies such as Buddhism and Jainism. An earlier tradition would place the Mahābhārata War c. 900 BC, according to which the 1,200 years of the Kali-yuga, if read as human years and not as 'years of the gods', would at this time be nearing their end. Evidently some pious Hindus thought that the dissolution of the cosmos was imminent. Perhaps it is to the departure of this fear in later times that we must attribute the devising of the 'years of the gods', which made the dissolution of the world comfortably distant.[185]

We need only refer to the remarks about the Boar Incarnation made earlier to see the force of the point. It is also worth noting that after political stability was restored in North India under Gupta rule, the tradition of maintaining archives was also revived. According to the usually dependable testimony of Xuanzang (Hiuen Tsiang) who visited India in the seventh century, detailed records were kept in each district during the reign of King Harṣa. These too have vanished—perhaps for the same reason as the Mauryan. It is worth recalling that by the twelfth century the two major universities of ancient India, those of Taxila and Nalanda had disappeared. An example might help make the point. What prospect would we hold out for British historiography in the future, if the universities of Oxford and Cambridge were utterly destroyed today along with all the libraries.

One could offer the sensational conclusion that the claim that the Hindus lacked a sense of history may itself indicate a lack of a sense of history on our part—for to make such a claim is to overlook the fact that the very evidence that demonstrates the Hindus possess it may have been lost on account of historical vicissitudes. But it is best to conclude on the sober note: that the proposition—that the Hindus lacked historical sense—is rendered questionable by the weight of the cumulative evidence presented above.

End Notes

1. D. C. Sircar, *Early Indian Numismatic and Epigraphical Studies* (Calcutta: Indian Museum, 1977), p. 91.

2. Vincent A. Smith, *The Oxford History of India From the Earliest Times to the End of 1911* (Oxford: Clarendon Press, 1923), p. xvi–xvii. The passage has been retained intact in Percival Spear, ed., *The Oxford History of India by the Late Vincent A. Smith C.I.E.* (fourth edition) (Delhi: Oxford University Press, 1994 [1981]), p. 13.

3. Vincent A. Smith, op. cit., p. xvii; Percival Spear, ed., op. cit., p. 13.

4. See D. C. Sircar, *Studies in the Geography of Ancient and Medieval India* (Delhi: Motilal Banarsidass, 1971), pp. 1–2.

5. A. L. Basham, *The Wonder That Was India* (New Delhi: Rupa & Co., 1999 [1954]), p. 62.

6. Hemchandra Raychaudhuri, *Political History of Ancient India, Commentary by B.N. Mukherjee* (Delhi: Oxford University Press, 1999), p. 431.

7. J. N. Banerjea, 'The Satraps of Northern and Western India', in K. A. Nilakanta Sastri, ed., *A Comprehensive History of India* (Bombay: Orient Longmans, 1957), p. 282.

8. P. V. Kane, *History of Dharmaśāstra* (Poona: Bhandarkar Oriental Research Institute, 1973), Vol. III, p. 30.

9. J.N. Banerjea, op. cit., p. 282. Also see Hemchandra Raychaudhuri, op. cit., p. 752.

10. Ibid., p. 281.

11. A. L. Basham, op. cit., p. 124.

12. D. C. Sircar, 'The Śaka Satraps of Western India', in R. C. Majumdar, ed., *The Age of Imperial Unity* (Bombay: Bharatiya Vidya Bhavan, 1968), p. 183.

13. J.N. Banerjea, op. cit., p. 282. Diacritics added. For Sanskrit text, see P.V. Kane, op. cit., Vol. III, p. 89: *sarva-kṣatrāviṣkṛta-vīraśabda-jātotsekāvidheyānāṁ yaudheyānāṁ prasahyotsādakena*.

14. A. L. Basham, op. cit., pp. 97–8.

15. Hemchandra Raychaudhuri, op. cit., p. 617, see also p. 601.

16. D. C. Sircar, 'The Śaka Satraps of Western India', op. cit., p. 184.

17. A. L. Basham, op. cit., p. 100; Hartmut Scharfe, *The State in Indian Tradition* (Leiden: E. J. Brill, 1989), p. 152.

18. A. L. Basham, op. cit., p. 99.

19. The cycle is repeated but *not* replicated, see Lynn Thomas, 'The Nature of the Repetition in the Indian Idea of Cyclical Times', in Peter Connolly and Sue Hamilton, eds, *Indian Insights: Buddhism, Brahmanism and Bhakti* (London: Luzac Oriental, 1997), pp. 83–9.

20. P. V. Kane, op. cit., Vol. III, p. 890.

21. Ibid.

22. D. C. Sircar, 'The Śaka Satraps of Western India', op. cit., p. 185.

23. Hemchandra Raychaudhuri, op. cit., p. 745.

24. J. N. Banerjea, op. cit., p. 282. Does the case of Skandagupta of the Gupta

dynasty provide a partial parallel here? (See Rama Shankar Tripathi, *History of Ancient India* [Delhi: Motilal Banarsidass, 1967], p. 260).

25. The claim could also contain a conventional element, see D. C. Sircar, *Studies in the Geography of Ancient and Medieval India*, p. 8.

26. Ram Sharan Sharma, *Śūdras in Ancient India* (New Delhi: Motilal Banarsidass, 1980 [1958]), p. 241.

27. Ibid., p. 330.

28. D. C. Sircar, *Studies in the Religious Life of Ancient and Medieval India* (Delhi: Motilal Banarsidass, 1971), p. 187: 'The Pala Emperors, who ruled in Bengal and Bihar from the eighth to the twelfth century, claimed to have been staunch followers of the Buddhist faith (*parama-saugata*). It is, however, interesting to note that, like typically zealous kings avowing the Brahmanical faith, the Palas were eager to suppress the social evil styled *varṇa-saṅkara*'.

29. A. L. Basham, op. cit., p. 415.

30. Hartmut Scharfe, op. cit., p. 124, note 773.

31. D. C. Sarkar, 'The Śaka Satraps of Western India', op. cit., p. 185.

32. P. V. Kane, op. cit., Vol. III, p. 197.

33. D. C. Sircar, *Studies in the Geography of Ancient and Medieval India*, p. 2.

34. Rama Shankar Tripathi, op. cit., p. 262.

35. The history of the pillar itself deserves separate treatment, see John Keay, *India: A History* (New York: Atlantic Monthly Press, 2000), pp. 136–7: 'Only under their son Samudra-Gupta does the dynasty emerge from obscurity. Like Kharavela's, it advances extravagant claims, but, like Rudradāman's, these claims are substantiated by other epigraphic and numismatic evidence. The inscription is probably the most famous in all India. Written in a script known as Gupta Brahmi (more elaborate than Ashoka Brahmi), and composed in classical Sanskrit verse and prose, its translation is often credited to James Prinsep of Ashoka fame, although it had been known and partially translated by earlier scholars. Its idiom and language echo that of Rudradāman. So does Samudra-Gupta's choice of site; for as if aspiring to Mauryan hegemony, his panegyric appears as an addition to the Edicts of Ashoka on one of those highly polished Ashokan pillars.

The pillar stands in the city of Allahabad where, soon after Prinsep's death, another Ashokan pillar, or part of it, was found in the possession of a contractor who used it as a road-roller. British antiquarians were mortified. A similar fate had almost befallen the pillar with the Samudra-Gupta epigraph. It had been uprooted in the eighteenth century and was discovered by Prinsep's colleagues lying half-buried in the ground. They re-erected it on a new pedestal and designed an Achaemenid-style replacement for its missing capital. Supposedly a lion, the capital 'resembles nothing so much as a stuffed poodle on top of an inverted flower pot,' wrote Alexander Cunningham, the father of Indian archaeology in the nineteenth century.

Cunningham also deduced that the Allahabad column had been shifted once before. Evidently later Muslim rulers had come to see these spectacular monoliths as a challenge to the excellence both of their sovereignty and their transport. They had therefore attempted to relocate them as totemic embellishments to their palatial courts. The truncated pillar which now tops Feroz Shah's palace in Delhi originally stood near Khizrabad higher up the Jamuna. A contemporary (thirteenth century) account describes how it was toppled onto a capacious pillow, then manoeuvred onto a forty-two-wheeler cart and hauled to the river by 8400 men. Lashed to a fleet of river transports, it was finally brought to Delhi in triumph.

Just so, the Allahabad pillar had apparently been shifted downriver from its original site in Kaushambi. It was meant to enhance the pretensions of the Allahabad fort as rebuilt by the Mughal emperor Akbar in the late sixteenth century. Akbar's son Jahangir would add his own inscription to those of Ashoka and Samudra-Gupta; and thus it is that scions of each of north India's three greatest dynasties—Maurya, Gupta and Mughal—share adjacent column inches in the heart of Allahabad, a city whose further claim to fame is as the home of a fourth great dynasty, that of the Nehru-Gandhis'.

36. Hemchandra Raychaudhuri, op. cit., pp. 470, 487.

37. Rama Shankar Tripathi, op. cit., p. 241. Also see Sadhu Ram, 'Allahabad Pillar Inscription of Samudragupta', in Mohan Chand, ed., *Ancient Indian Culture and Literature (Pt. Ganga Ram Commemoration Volume)* (Delhi: Eastern Book Linkers, 1980), pp. 131–3.

38. Ibid., p. 240.

39. R. C. Majumdar, 'The Foundation of the Gupta Empire', in R. C. Majumdar, ed., *The Classical Age* (Bombay: Bharatiya Vidya Bhavan, 1970 [1954]), p. 7. Hemchandra Raychaudhuri also compares him to Aśoka (op. cit., pp. 485–6): 'Samudra Gupta favoured poetry as well as the Śāstra, while Aśoka seems to have specialized in scriptural studies alone. The former undertook military campaigns with the object of *sarva-pṛithivī-jaya*, conquest of the whole earth, as known to his panegyrist, the latter eschewed military conquest after the Kaliṅga war and organized missions to effect *Dhamma-vijaya*, conquest of the hearts of men, in three continents. Yet in spite of these differences there was much that was common to these remarkable men. Both laid stress on *parākrama*, ceaseless exertion in the cause in which they believed. Both expressed solicitude for the people committed to their care, and were kind even to vanquished enemies. And both laid emphasis on *Dharma*. Samudra Gupta no less than Dharmāśoka, made firm the rampart of the true law (*Dharma-prāchīra-bandhaḥ*)'.

40. Rama Shankar Tripathi, op. cit., p. 241; for another view see John Keay, op. cit., p. 137l.

41. Hemchandra Raychaudhuri, op. cit., p. 471.

42. Rama Shankar Tripathi, op. cit., p. 242. Although 'the dominions of ... five kings, viz. Rudradeva, Matila, Nāgadatta, Nandin, and Balavarman cannot be located at present. We can form an idea of the territory thus conquered ...' (R. C. Majumdar, op. cit., p. 8).

43. Hemchandra Raychaudhuri, op. cit., p. 474, note 1.

44. Ram Sharan Sharma, op. cit., p. 160; also see R. P. Kangle, *The Kauṭilīya Arthaśāstra* (Delhi: Motilal Banarsidass, 1988 [965]), Pt III, p. 74.

45. R. C. Majumdar, op. cit., p. 9.

46. Hemchandra Raychaudhuri, op. cit., p. 475.

47. Ibid., p. 473.

48. Rama Shankar Tripathi, op. cit., pp. 242–3.

49. Ibid.

50. R. C. Majumdar, op. cit., p. 10.

51. Ibid., p. 243.

52. Mālavas, Ārjunāyana, Yaudheya, Madraka, Ābhīra, Prārjuna, Sanakānīka, Kāka, and Kharaparikas (ibid., pp. 244–5).

53. Samataṭa (South-Eastern Bengal); Ḍavāka (Dacca); Kāmarūpa (Assam); Nepal and Karṭṛpura (ibid., p. 244).

54. R. C. Majumdar, op. cit., p. 8.

55. Ibid., p. 11.

56. Rama Shankar Tripathi, op. cit., p. 247.

57. Hartmut Scharfe, *The State in Indian Tradition* (Leiden: E. J. Brill, 1989), p. 63, note 293; Rama Shankar Tripathi, op. cit., p. 240.

58. Hartmut Scharfe, op. cit., p. 56.

59. Hemchandra Raychaudhuri, op. cit., p. 484: 'In the Poona plates Samudra Gupta receives the epithet *anekāśvamedhayājin*. He was believed to have celebrated more than one horse-sacrifice. Some of the campaigns described in the Allahabad panegyric may have been actually conducted by Princes or officers who kept guard over the sacrificial horse that was allowed to roam at large. In the inscription of Harisheṇa the credit for capturing some of the vanquished chieftains is given to the army. Among the great commanders were men like Tilabhaṭṭaka and Harisheṇa himself, who was the son of Dhruvabhūti'.

60. Ibid., p. 47.

61. Ibid. pp. 478–9: 'The absence of any clear reference to Pṛithivīsheṇa I in Harisheṇa's Praśasti is explained by the fact that Samudragupta's operations were actually confined to the eastern part of Trans-Vindhyan India. There is no reliable evidence that the Gupta conqueror carried his arms to the central and western parts of the Deccan proper, i.e. to the territory ruled by Pṛithivīsheṇa I itself. Professor Dubreuil has shown that the identification of Devarāshtra with Mahārāshṭra and the Eranḍapalla with Eranḍol in Khandesh is probably wrong.

Though Samudragupta did not invade the Western Deccan it is clear from his Eraṇ Inscription that he did deprive the Vākāṭakas of their possessions in Central India. These territories were not, however, directly governed by the Vākāṭaka monarch, but were under a vassal prince. In the time of Pṛithivīsheṇa this prince was Vyāghra. We should naturally expect a conflict between the Vākāṭaka feudatory and the Gupta conqueror. Curiously enough, the Allahabad Praśasti refers to Samudragupta's victory over Vyāghrarāja of Mahākāntāra. It is probable that this Vyāghrarāja is identical with the Vyāghra of the Nāchnā Inscription who was the Central Indian feudatory the Guptas succeeded the Vākāṭakas as the paramount power in parts of Central India. Henceforth the Vākāṭakas appear in fact as a purely southern power'.

62. R. C. Majumdar, op. cit., p. 7.

63. Hartmut Scharfe, op. cit., p. 64.

64. R. C. Majumdar, op. cit., p. 7.

65. Hemchandra Raychaudhuri, op. cit., p. 470.

66. R. C. Majumdar, *Ancient India* (Delhi: Motilal Banarsidass, 1964), p. 231.

67. John Keay, op. cit., p. 137.

68. Hemchandra Raychaudhuri, op. cit., p. 482, note 9.

69. Percival Spear ed., op. cit., p. 224.

70. K. Satchidananda Murty, *Revelation and Reason in Advaita Vedānta*, (Delhi: Motilal Banarsidass, 1974), p. 217.

71. Ibid.

72. Vasudeva Sharana Agrawala, 'Yāska and Pāṇini', in Haridas Bhattacharyya, ed., *The Cultural Heritage of India* (Calcutta: The Ramakrishna Mission Institute of Culture, 1958), Vol. I, pp. 293–301.

73. Ibid., p. 294.

74. K. Satchidananda Murty, *Vedic Hermeneutics* (Delhi: Motilal Banarsidass, 1993), p. 12.

75. Ibid., p. 11.

76. Ibid., p. 29.

77. Ibid., p. 67, note 30.

78. T. M. P. Mahadevan, *Outlines of Hinduism* (Bombay: Chetana Limited, 1971), p. 138.

79. K. Satchidananda Murty, *Reason and Revelation in Advaita Vedānta,* p. 42.

80. Ibid., p. 45.

81. Michael Witzel, op. cit., pp. 5–6.

82. Ainslie T. Embree, ed., *The Hindu Tradition* (New York: Random House, 1972), p. 220.

83. Anindita Balslev, *A Study of Time in Indian Philosophy* (Wiesbaden: Otto Harrassowitz, 1983).

84. P. V. Kane, op. cit., Vol. III, p. 890.

85. W. Norman Brown, *Man in the Universe: Some Continuities in Indian Thought* (Berkeley and Los Angeles: University of California Press, 1966), p. 75.

86. Michael Witzel, op. cit., p. 42, note 22: 'Though the origin of the universe is somewhat shrouded in mystery, time never began nor will it ever end: instead, it moves in cycles: The first cycle of creation of this world and the following cycles, called *yugas*, lead up to still later ones (already hinted at in RV 8.87.4). Just like the *yugas* which follow each other in endless succession, so behave the sun, the moon and the stars: the succession of dawn and dusk, day and night, new moon and full moon, the 3 to 6 seasons of the year, the bright half of the year "when the sun moves northwards" and dark half of the year, the return of the new year as such at winter solstice, the counter-clockwise turning of the Milky Way around the north pole during the course of the year,—as well as a five year cycle (originally called *dyumna*, i.e., the period after which solar and lunar months can be made to start over again at the same point in time) all point to the cyclical nature of time. The dangerous

transition points to this process are clearly marked by Vedic rituals, as well as the human rites of passage, in the cycle of birth, death and rebirth'.

87. Michael Witzel, op. cit., p. 6.

88. Ibid.

89. P. V. Kane, op. cit., Vol. II, Pt I, p. 33.

90. A. L. Basham, *The Wonder That Was India*, p. 148.

91. Ibid., p. 146.

92. Michael Witzel, op. cit., p. 36.

93. Ibid., p. 3.

94. Ibid.

95. M. K. Gandhi, *Hindu Dharma*, edited by Bhartan Kumarappa (Ahmedabad: Navajivan Press, 1958), p. 234.

96. Michael Witzel, op. cit., p. 4.

97. Ibid., p. 4.

98. A. L. Basham, op. cit., p. 149.

99. Michael Witzel, op. cit., p. 9.

100. See Satyaketu Vidyalankara, *Origine et histoire de la caste vaiśya Agrawals* (Paris: Adrien-Maisonneuve, 1938). According to Hyla S. Converse: 'The material refers to the fact that the Agrawals were originally (according to the ancient material of their *bhāṭs*) in enmity with Indra and worshipped a mother goddess with great bloody sacrifices. In a battle with Indra they were defeated, and the agreement reached was that their religion would henceforth be controlled and directed by brahmins, their kingly family would be incorporated into Indra's community but only at the rank of *vaiśyas* (not *kṣatriyas*), and that the rest of their people would be *śūdras* (because of their sins. No sins of the people had been mentioned until this point in the story). The author of the study had gathered his material from recitations of *vaiśya* Agrawal *bhāṭs*'. (Hyla S. Converse and Arvind Sharma 'Ancient Śūdra Account of the Origin of Castes', *Journal of the American Oriental Society 114.4* [1994], p. 642).

101. Michael Witzel, op. cit., p. 36.

102. Hyla S. Converse and Arvind Sharma, op. cit., pp. 642–3.

103. Ibid., p. 643.

104. A. L. Basham, op. cit., pp. 4, 44.

105. J. W. McCrindle, *Ancient India As Described by Megasthenes and Arrian* (revised second edition) (Calcutta: Chuckervertty, Chatterjee & Co., 1860 [1876–7]), pp. 115–16;

106. Ibid., p. 208.

107. Edward C. Sachau, op. cit., Pt II, p. 1.

108. Ibid.

109. Ibid., Pt II, p. 42.

110. Ibid.

111. Michael Witzel, op. cit., pp. 28–9.

112. Ibid., pp. 21–9.

113. A. L. Basham, op. cit., p. 493

114. Padmanabh S. Jaini, *The Jaina Path of Purification* (Berkeley: University of California Press, 1979), pp. 37–8, emphasis added.

115. Ibid., p. 38, note 88.

116. K. A. Nilakanta Sastri and G. Srinivasachari, *Advanced History of India* (Bombay: Allied Publishers, 1971), p. 65.

117. K. S. Ch'en, Buddhism: *The Light of Asia* (Hauppauge, New York: Barron's Educational Series Inc., 1968), pp. 13–15. Also see R. C. Majumdar, ed., *The Age of Imperial Unity* (Bombay: Bharatiya Vidya Bhavan, 1968), pp. 36–8, 92–4.

118. Ibid., p. 36

119. A. L. Basham, (op. cit., pp. 493–4) lists (1) Era of the Kaliyuga (3102 BC); (2) Śrī Laṅkan Buddha Era (544 BC); (3) Era of Mahāvīra (528 BC); (4) Vikrama Era (58 BC); (5) Śaka Era (78 AD); (6) Licchavi Era (110 AD); (7) Kalacūrī Era (248 AD); (8) Gupta Era (320 AD); (9) Harṣa Era (606 AD); (10) Kollam Era of Malabār (825 AD); (11) Nevār Era (878 AD) (12) Era of Vikramāditya VI Cālukya (1075 AD); (13) Lakṣmaṇa Era of Bengal (1119 AD). A. L. Basham also mentions the *saptarṣi*, or Laukika Era of Kashmir as belonging to the Middle Ages but does not specify the initial year. Al-Bīrūnī (Edward C. Sachau, op. cit., Pt I, p. 1ff) lists the following Eras: (1) the beginning of the existence of the day of the present Nychthemeron of Brahman, i.e., the beginning of the Kalpa; (3) the Manvantara, in which we are now; (4) the beginning of the twenty-eighth Caturyuga, in which we are now; (5) the beginning of the fourth Yuga of the present Caturyuga; (6) Pāṇḍava-Kāla, i.e. the time of the life and the wars of Bhārata; (7) Śrī Harṣa Era; (8) Vikramāditya Era; (9) Śaka Era; (10) Valabha Era; (11) Gupta Era; (12) Era of the canon of *Khaṇḍa-Khādyaka*; (13) Era of the canon of *Pañcasiddhāntikā* of Varāhamihira; (14) Era of the canon of *Karaṇasāra*; (15) Era of the canon of *Karaṇa-tilaka*. Michael Witzel (op. cit., p. 36) refers additionally to a Śūdraka Saṁvat (170 BC) and Mānadeva Saṁvat (576 AD). Hemchandra Raychaudhuri also refers to a Muriya-Kāla or Mauryan Era (op. cit., p. 334, note 1).

120. D. Devahuti, op. cit., p. 235

121. Cited, ibid., p. 236

122. Ibid.

123. Ibid., p. 236

124. Ibid., pp. 236–7

125. Edward C. Sachau, tr., *Alberuni's India* (London: Kegan Paul, Trench, Trubner & Co., 1914), Pt II, pp. 1, 7. He subsequently seems to mention four others, ibid.

126. Edward C. Sachau, tr., op. cit., Pt II, p. 178.

127. See Arvind Sharma, '"Alberuni's India" as a Source of Political History', *Central Asian Journal* 23:1–2 (1982), pp. 131–6.

128. That one may have to rely on epigraphic rather than documentary material in this context would not have surprised Megasthenes who 'observed the much greater part played by oral tradition and memory, as compared with *written* documents, though he cannot have asserted that writing is unknown, as Strabo would seem to imply, since in one passage he refers to written inscriptions' (E. R. Bevan, 'India in

Early Greek and Latin Literature', in E. J. Rapson, ed., *Ancient India* [(Cambridge: Cambridge University Press, 1922], p. 413, emphasis added).

129. Michael Witzel, op. cit., p. 9.

130. R. P. Kangle, *The Kauṭilīya Arthaśāstra* (Delhi: Motilal Banarsidass, 1988 [1965], Pt III, p. 201): 'An office of very great importance, situated in the capital, is the *akṣapaṭala*. It is a sort of records-cum-audit office. There is an *adhyakṣa* in charge, with a special building of his own with many halls and record rooms (2.7.1). The records to be maintained there pertain to (1) the activity of each state department, (2) the working of state factories and conditions governing production in them, (3) prices, samples and standards of measuring instruments for various kinds of goods, (4) laws, transactions, customs, and regulations in force in different regions, villages, castes, families and corporations, (5) salaries and other perquisites of state servants, (6) what is made over to the king and other members of the royal family, and (7) payments made to and amounts received from foreign princes, whether allies or foes (2.7.2). A more comprehensive record-house can hardly be thought of'.

131. Hartmut Scharfe, op. cit., p. 139.

132. See P.V. Kane, op. cit., Vol. III, pp. 308–12. 'Yāj. II. 84–94, Nār. IV. 69–75 and 135–46, Bṛ., Kāt. 249–312, Śukra II. 291–318, IV. 172–82 and several digests devote great attention to documents. A few salient points only will be brought out here. Nār. (IV. 70–1) eulogises documents by saying that if the Creator had not created writing which is like an excellent eye, the world would have come to grief and that a document is an indubitable means of apprehending the time, the place, the object, the material, the extent and the duration of a transaction. Bṛ. (q. in V.P. p. 141) says that, since people begin to entertain doubts (about a transaction) even in six months (from an occurrence or transaction) the Creator therefore created in the hoary past letters which are recorded on writing material (*patra*). The Lalitavistara (about 2nd or 3rd century AD) mentions 64 scripts which were known to the Buddha among which the first is Brāhmī (10th chap. p. 143). Nār., Bṛ., and Śukra probably try to explain why the alphabet current in their days was called Brāhmī (it was created by Brahmā). Śukra II. 297, IV. 5. 172 are similar verses. The texts divide documents in different ways. Viṣṇu Dh.S. VII.2 divides documents into three kinds viz. those written before the king (i.e. by public officers), those bearing the superscription of witnesses and those without witnesses. The first is a document written in a state office by a scribe appointed by the king and bearing the signature of the head or superintendent of the office. This is just like the registration of documents in modern India. Bṛ. (q. by V.P. p. 141, V. May, p. 24) divides documents into three sorts viz. royal writing, writing made at a fixed place and that written in one's own hand. Nār. IV.135 speaks of two kinds viz. one written by the executant himself in his own hand and that written by another; (the first of these is valid) without attesting witnesses, while the second requires to be attested. In the former no writer (lekhaka) nor witnesses are necessary, while in the latter both are necessary. Even now in India no deed concerning even immoveable property is required by law to be attested except mortgages and gifts. The author of the Sangraha, the Mit. on Yaj. II. 84 and several others divide documents into rājakīya (public) and *jānapada* (private or of the

common people). The V. Mayukha (p. 24) says that *laukika* and *jānapada* are synonyms and *jānapada* document is of two kinds viz. written by the executant himself in his own hand and that written by another, and that the first may be without attestation of witnesses, but the other must be attested. On Yāj. II 22 the Mit. divides documents into śāsana and cīraka. The first is the same as rājakīya (described in Yāj. I. 318–20) and cīraka is practically the same as jānapada writing. On Yāj. II 89 the Mit. remarks that a royal deed must be written in correct and elegant language but a document executed by ordinary people is not required to be in correct Sanskrit, but may be written in the local dialect of the parties. Yāj. II. 89 states that a document written by the executant himself in his own hand is authoritative except when it is brought about by force or fraud. Yāj. II. 84–7 prescribe that a document of debt or the like should be written down by mutual agreement, that the creditor's name should be placed first, that it should mention the year, month, half month, *tithi* (day), the names, caste, gotras, the Vedic School, the names of the fathers of the parties, that when the writing is finished the debtor should write at the end that the deed is approved by N. N. (the executant) son of so and so, that an even number (i.e. not less than two) should attest the document, stating their father's names and that they attest as witnesses and the scribe should write at the end that he wrote the document at the request of both parties. If the debtor, or any witness cannot write, his signature should be made by another in the presence of all witnesses (Nār, q. by Mit. on Yāj. II. 87 and by the Vy. Nir. p. 87 without name). Rājakīya documents are of three kinds (acc. to Br. quoted in V.P. p. 141, V. May. p. 24) viz. *śāsana* (a royal grant of land), *jayapatra* (a judgement deciding a law suit) *prasāda-patra* (a deed showing the king's pleasure at the devoted service or bravery of a person); acc. to Vasiṣṭha (q. in Sim. C. II. P. 55 and V. May p. 28) it is four kinds viz. *śāsana*, *jayapatra*, *ājñātra* (a royal command addressed to feudatories, high or low officers like the wardens of the marches), *prajñāpanāpatra* (a writing of request addressed by the king to sacrificial priest, a purohita, teacher, learned brāhmaṇas or other highly honoured persons); it is five-fold acc. to S.V. pp. 111–13 viz. śāsana, jayapatra, ājñāpatra, prajñāpanāpatra and prasādapatra. Kaut. in II. 10 speaks of several kinds of royal orders and names them, such as prajñāpana (request by a messenger about what another prays), ājñ āpatra (as above), *paridāna* (honour to the deserving or gift in distress), *parihāra* (remission of taxes for certain castes or villages by the king), *nisṛṣṭilekha* (writing whereby the king accepts the actions or words of some trustworthy person as his own), *prāvṛttika* (conveying information about some portentous happening or some news about enemies etc,) *pratilekha* (reply in accordance with discussion held with the king on a message from another), *sarvatraga* (order addressed to high functionaries and officers for the welfare of travellers). The contents and form of royal grants have been described in H. of Dh. Vol. II pp. 860–1. The jānapada writings are divided into various sorts, seven (acc. to Br. q. by Aparārka p. 683, Sm. C.II. p. 60) or eight (acc. to Vyāsa in Sm. C. II. p. 59) and the Sm. C. remarks that there is no emphasis on the number and there may be many more varieties'.

133. 'The King issued edicts (śāsana) which contained commands, edicts for instance for Śvapāka etc. (X.55). Forging a royal edict was a grave offence (IX.332).

There were records kept in government record offices. Decisions of village disputes were entered into them for future integrity (nibandhanīyāt; VIII.255)'. (V.S. Agrawala, *India As Described by Manu* [Varanasi: Prithvi Prakashan, 1970], p. 50).

134. Hemchandra Raychaudhuri, op. cit., p. 482.

135. Samuel Beal, tr., op. cit., p. 78: 'With respect to the records of events, each province has its own official for preserving them in writing. The record of these events in their full character is called Ni-lo-pi-ch'a (Nīlapiṭa, blue deposit). In these records are mentioned good and evil events, with calamities and fortunate occurances'.

136. The care which apparently went into the preparation of some of these documents makes their loss all the more painful. A. L. Basham writes (op. cit., p. 100): 'To transmit the royal decrees a corps of secretaries and clerks was maintained, and remarkable precautions were taken to prevent error. Under the Cōḻas, for instance, orders were first written by scribes at the king's dictation, and the accuracy of the drafts was attested by competent witnesses. Before being sent to their recipients they were carefully transcribed, and a number of witnesses, sometimes amounting to as many as [illegible]teen, again attested them. In the case of grants of land and privileges an important court official was generally deputed to ensure that the royal decrees were put into effect. Thus records were kept with great care, and nothing was left to chance; the royal scribes themselves were often important personages'.

137. Michael Witzel, op. cit., p. 44, note 35.

138. Michael Witzel, op. cit., p. 38.

139. Ibid., p. 39.

140. Ibid., p. 38.

141. Ibid., p. 8.

142. Ibid., p. 8. A certain sense for history is evinced even in sacrificial literature. U. N. Ghoshal notes: 'On the day of loosening of the sacrificial horse, the hotri priest recites to the crowned king surrounded by his sons and ministers what are called the 'revolving' (or recurring) legends (pāriplava ākhyāna). These are so called because the priest recites on ten successive days as many different Vedas, and this goes on for a year in cycles of ten days each. In the order of this narration Itihāsa and Purāṇa are reserved for the eighth and nineth days, while Rik. Yajus, Atharvan, Angirasa, sarpa-vidyā ('the science of snakes'), devjñāna-vidyā (knowledge of divine beings), māyā (magic) are mentioned for the first seven days, and Sāman for the tenth'. *Studies in Indian History and Culture* [Bombay: Orient Longmans, 1965], p. 12).

143. The full title of his well-known work is revealing: *Political History of Ancient India From the Accession of Parikshit to the Extinction of the Gupta Dynasty*.

144. Michael Witzel, op. cit., p. 12.

145. Ibid.

146. Romila Thapar, *Ancient Indian Social History: Some Interpretations* (New Delhi: Orient Longman, 1978), p. 278.

147. Michael Witzel, op. cit., p. 37.

148. Romila Thapar, op. cit., p. 278. Romila Thapar writes (op. cit., p. 281): 'The

Puranic myth referring to the origin of the two royal lineage has a fairly obvious meaning. The great flood caused the total destruction of the world and this is a recognized stage in the cyclic time concept. The beginnings of history therefore emerge from a condition which has no antecedents: it is in fact symbolic of the very beginning. The birth of the two royal lines from a hermaphrodite suggests a variation of the idea of twins as parents, indicating the purity of the lineage. The choice of the two lineage names—the Sun and the Moon—is equally significant. Perhaps a structuralist would see in this the bi-polarity of male and female, day and night, and a series of other opposed pairs. Perhaps the myth was a memory of the dividing of the tribes into two rival groups. Alternatively, it was an attempt to weave the many dynastic strands into two main currents and finally to a single origin. It is not surprising that the word Manu provided the generic base for *mānava* meaning "mankind".'

149. F. E. Pargiter, *Ancient Indian Historical Tradition* (London: Milford, 1922); see *The Purana Text of the Dynasties of Kali Age* (Oxford: Oxford University Press, 1913).

150. For a useful summary account see R. C. Majumdar, op. cit., pp. 68–73.

151. Michael Witzel, op. cit., pp. 40–1: 'The Yāyu Purāṇa (I.31-32) expressly lays down "the sūta's special duty, as received by good men of old, was to preserve the genealogies of gods, *ṛṣis* (sages) and most glorious kings, and traditions of great men"' (Shankar Goyal, *History Writing of Early India: New Discoveries and Approaches* [Jodhpur: Kusumanjali Prakashan, 1996], p. 9).

152. Romila Thapar, op. cit., p. 291.

153. See Chandra Prabha, *Historical Mahākāvyas in Sanskrit (Eleventh to Fifteenth Century)* (New Delhi: Shri Bharat Bharati Pvt., Ltd., 1976).

154. Michael Witzel, op. cit., p. 5.

155. Ibid., p. 38.

156. A. L. Basham, op. cit., p. 424.

157. Julie Hamper Hiebert, 'Royal Evenings: Sanskrit Poetry of Queen and Court', doctoral dissertation, Department of Sanskrit and Indian Studies, Harvard University, 1988.

158. V. S. Agrawala, 'Yāska and Pāṇini', in Haridas Bhattacharyya, ed., *The Cultural Heritage of India* (Calcutta: The Ramakrishna Mission Institute of Culture, 1958), Vol. I, p. 283.

159. Michael Witzel, op. cit., p. 3.

160. Rama Shankar Tripathi, op. cit., pp. 185–6.

161. 'The authors of the astronomical works generally also give the exact date of the day on which they completed their work' (Maurice Winternitz, *A History of Indian Literature* [Calcuttta: University of Calcutta, 1927], p. 30). Aryabhatta tells us his precise age.

162. F. J. Staal, ed., *A Reader on the Sanskrit Grammarians* (Cambridge, Massachusetts, and London, England: The MIT Press, 1972), p. 78.

163. Michael Witzel, op. cit., pp. 38–9: 'Due to the particularly good situation with regard to historical documentation in Nepal we not only know who composed

them and when, but we even know when they were first performed and by whom: 'In NS 503, on Pauṣa *kṛṣṇa ekādaśī* the drama Bhairavānanda was inaugurated. After 24 days of rehearsal and practice, on the day of Māgha *kṛṣṇa daśamī*, the *siddhi phaye* ceremony was completed in Śrī Kothocheṃ. This drama was written by Manaku Bhā (Maṇikya Vardhana) of Yambaṭunam Vihāra, by consulting the work written in the Ḍoya (Deva, Sanskrit) language. The brother of Manaku Bhā, Ujhājīva Bhāro's head was decorated with a *gajura* and a head dress for dance. (The crown prince) Śrīśrī-Dharmamalladeva Ṭhākura had contributed to this work. This play was written for Ṭhākura's marriage. The marriage took place on Thursday, Phālguṇa śukla tṛtīya, evening. The persons in charge of staging the play were Śrī Dvijarāja Bhāro, Jyoti Kasta Bhā, and Gajā Mulāmi. The play was staged all over the three principalities. All participated in the dance. (transl. Malla, fol. 62)'. He goes on to say: 'Many of these dramas survive. They are written in a mixture of Sanskrit, Old Newari and Old Maithili. The latter two languages replace Prakrits of the classical dramas. This new tradition was carried on during the later Malla period as well, and Pratāpamalla of Kathmandu (1641–74) called himself a Kavindra. Accordingly, he set up an inscription at the royal palace at Vasantapur (Kathmandu) which shows his supreme knowledge of 'all languages'. Indeed, the inscription also contains the two French words, incised in the florid Roman letters of the period, 'L'AUTOMNE L'HIVERE'. These dramas still are occasionally performed today, one of them has now been edited and studied in detail by H. Brinkhaus (Stuttgart, 1987)'.

164. Harinath De, *Select Papers Mainly Indological* (Calcutta: Sanskrit Pustak Bhandar, 1972), pp. 155–6.

165. H. C. Raychaudhuri, op. cit., p. 477.

166. Steven J. Gelberg, ed., *Hare Krishna, Hare Krishna: Five Distinguished Scholars on the Krishna Movement in the West* (New York: Grove Press Inc., 1983), pp. 211–14. Some time after reading this I happened to meet Shrivatsa Gosvami himself at the Centre for the Study of World Religions at Harvard University, during one of his trips to the United States. As soon as I saw him I made a beeline for him and asked him point blank: 'What did Professor Basham say?' He paused only fractionally before catching the reference almost immediately and began to laugh. Then he said: 'What could he say?' It bothered me that the pre-eminent Western cultural historian of Indic civilization should have nothing to say. But perhaps I am being unfair to him. Once, during my sojourn as a student at Harvard University, Professor D. H. H. Ingalls had repeated the remark about Hindus having no sense of history, at which I had tried to soften the blow, as it were, by citing obvious instances of it—such as the traditional account that during the reign of Nichakṣu, sixth in descent from King Parikshit, the city of Hastināpura was carried away by the Ganges, having been confirmed archeologically. (see H. C. Raychaudhuri, op. cit., p. 571). He then remarked that during the one talk Professor Basham delivered at Harvard, he had urged a revision of the standard view. So perhaps, like all scholars who adjust their views to evidence and not vice versa, he may have begun to rethink the matter.

167. Ibid., p. 15.

168. Heinrich von Stietencron, 'Political Aspects of Indian Religious Art', *Visible Religion* IV/V (1985/86), p. 16

169. Ibid., p. 18.

170. Percival Spear, ed., op. cit., pp. 214–15.

171. Heinrich von Stietencron, op. cit., p. 18.

172. A. L. Basham, op. cit., p. 371.

173. Hemchandra Raychaudhuri, op. cit., p. 165.

174. Heinrich von Stietencron, op. cit., p. 21.

175. Ibid.

176. Ibid.

177. E. R. Bevan, 'India in Early Greek and Latin Literature', in E. J. Rapson, ed., *Ancient India* (Cambridge: Cambridge University Press, 1922), p. 413.

178. P. V. Kane, *History of Dharmaśāstra* (Poona: Bhandarkar Oriental Research Institute, 1974), Voi. II, Pt. I, pp. 347–9, 370.

179. Edward C. Sachau, ed., *Alberuni's India* (London: Kegan Paul, Trench, Trubner & Co., 1914), Vol. I, p. 22.

180. A. S. Altekar, *The Position of Women in Hindu Civilization* (New Delhi: Motilal Banardisass, 1995), p. 350.

181. Ibid., p. 350.

182. Ram Sharan Sharma, op. cit., p. 193. Ram Sharan Sharma also finds evidence of this socio-economic crisis in a passage in the *Manusmṛti* (viii.418) when he writes (ibid.), 'At another place Manu ordains that the king should carefully compel the Vaiśyas and the Śūdras to perform the tasks assigned to them; since, if these two varnas swerve from their duties, they will throw the whole world into confusion. This passage is of particular importance, for it is not to be found in any earlier text'.

183. Hemchandra Raychaudhuri, op. cit., p. 324, note 3.

184. Hartmut Scharfẹ, *The State in Indian Tradition* (Leiden: E. J. Brill, 1989), p. 139, note 114.

185. A. L. Basham, op. cit., p. 321.

Index